PENGUIN BOOKS

SIMPLICITY

Edward de Bono has had faculty appointments at the universities of Oxford, London, Cambridge and Harvard. He is widely regarded as the leading authority in the direct teaching of thinking as a skill. He originated the concept of lateral thinking and developed formal techniques for deliberate creative thinking. He has written fifty-six books, which have been translated into thirty-four languages, has made two television series and there are over 4,000,000 references to his work on the Internet.

Dr de Bono has been invited to lecture in fifty-two countries and to address major international conferences. In 1989 he was asked to chair a special meeting of Nobel Prize laureates. His instruction in thinking has been sought by some of the leading business corporations in the world such as IBM, Du Pont, Shell, Eriksson, McKinseys, Ciba-Geigy, Ford and many others. He has had a planet named after him by the International Astronomic Union and was named by a group of university professors in South Africa as one of the 250 people in all of history who have contributed most to humanity.

Dr de Bono runs the most widely used programme for the direct teaching of thinking in schools. This is now in use in many countries around the world.

Dr de Bono's key contribution has been his understanding of the brain as a self-organizing system. From this solid base he set out to design practical tools for thinking. His work is in use equally in the boardrooms of some of the world's largest corporations and with four-year-olds in school. His design of the Six Hats method provides Western thinking, for the first time, with a constructive idiom instead of adversarial argument. His work is in use in élite gifted schools, rural schools in South Africa and Khmer villages in Cambodia. The appeal of Dr de Bono's work is its simplicity and practicality.

For more information about Dr de Bono's public seminars, private seminars, certified training programmes, thinking programmes for schools, CD Rom, books and tapes, please contact: Diane McQuaig, The McQuaig Group, 132 Rochester Avenue, Toronto M4N 1P1, Ontario, Canada. Tel: (416) 488 0008. Fax: (416) 488 4544. Internet: http://www.edwdebono.com/

Atlas of Management Thinking
Conflicts: A Better Way to Resolve Them
Edward de Bono's Masterthinker's Handbook
Edward de Bono's Textbook of Wisdom
The 5-Day Course in Thinking
Handbook for the Positive Revolution
The Happiness Purpose
How to be More Interesting
I Am Right You Are Wrong
Lateral Thinking
Lateral Thinking for Management
Opportunities
Parallel Thinking
Po: Beyond Yes and No
Practical Thinking
Simplicity
Six Thinking Hats
Teach Your Child How to Think
Teach Yourself to Think
Teaching Thinking
The Use of Lateral Thinking
Water Logic
Wordpower

Simplicity

Edward de Bono

PENGUIN BOOKS

PENGUIN BOOKS

Published by the Penguin Group
Penguin Books Ltd, 27 Wrights Lane, London W8 5TZ, England
Penguin Putnam Inc., 375 Hudson Street, New York, New York 10014, USA
Penguin Books Australia Ltd, Ringwood, Victoria, Australia
Penguin Books Canada Ltd, 10 Alcorn Avenue, Toronto, Ontario, Canada M4V 3B2
Penguin Books (NZ) Ltd, Private Bag 102902, NSMC, Auckland, New Zealand

Penguin Books Ltd, Registered Offices: Harmondsworth, Middlesex, England

First published by Viking 1998
Published in Penguin Books 1999
10 9 8 7 6 5 4 3 2 1

Cover concept suggested by Mary Pinnock

Set in Monotype Baskerville
Printed in England by Clays Ltd, St Ives plc

The ten rules of simplicity start on page 279. You can turn to page 279 to read these rules as an indication of what the book is going to be about. Or you can wait until you reach them, and they will give a summary of what has been in the book.

In an increasingly complex world 'simplicity' is becoming one of the four key values.

* Research shows that 95 per cent of people do not use 90 per cent of the features on their video-recorders – because they are too complicated. What can you tell about a family where the clock on the video-recorder is not flashing? They have a teenager in the house.

* In one country small businessmen have to cope with 16,000 laws in order to carry on their business.

* In another country the tax laws run to 40,000 pages.

* In another country the farmers rioted because they could not understand the new laws they were supposed to obey.

* It is said that Ken Olsen, the founder of DEC, once complained that at home he had a microwave oven that was so complex that he could not use it.

* In your own mind add further examples of the increasing complexity of the world around. Send such examples to me if you wish.

* An old woman spent a week in a shopping mall in Holland. She could not find her way out. She bought food during the day and slept on a bench at night.

* Instructions for machines, computers, etc., are always written by those who know the system and are not much help to those who do not. Have you ever seen a sign on a road reading: 'This is not the road to the airport.' Those who know the system cannot imagine the problems facing those who do not.

There is often a much simpler way of doing things – if you make the effort to look for it. Simplicity does not just happen.

Try out this simple arithmetic task:

1. Add up all the numbers from 1 to 10.

2. Add up all the numbers from 1 to 100.

Which of the two is the easiest to do?

Do your own thinking before turning to the next page.

Simplicity is easy to use but can be hard to design. You may need some creativity.

At first sight it seems obvious that adding up the numbers from 1 to 10 must be easier than adding up the numbers from 1 to 100. It is just a matter of adding the numbers together, one after the other, and getting the total of 55.

The addition of the numbers from 1 to 100 seems difficult because it is tedious and boring and you might make mistakes. So it is just possible that you may spend time trying to find a 'simpler' way of making the addition.

Spend some time doing just that before turning the page.

You have to want to look for simplicity. You have to be motivated to design simplicity. Whose business is it to make things more simple?

Imagine the numbers going up in a staircase from 1 to 100 as shown in diagram 1. The first step is one unit high, the second step is two units high, the third step is three units high . . . the hundredth step is one hundred units high. So if we added up all the steps we would be adding up all the numbers from one to one hundred.

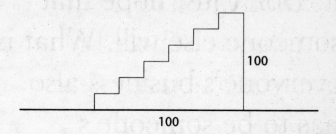

Now imagine a similar staircase placed upside-down over the first one. There has to be an overlap of one at the end in order to fit a similar staircase – as shown in diagram 2. We now have a rectangle which is 100 units along one side and 101 units along the other side. To get the total area we just multiply 100 × 101. That would give us 'twice' the total we need because we have added up 'two' staircases so we divide by two. The answer is 5,050.

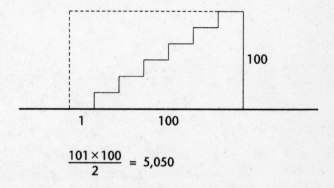

$$\frac{101 \times 100}{2} = 5{,}050$$

If something needs doing, then do something about it. Don't just hope that someone else will. What is everyone's business also has to be someone's business.

Suggestion 1

Every country should set up a National Institute for Simplicity

Of course, such an institute might quickly become bureaucratic and complex. At the same time, things rarely happen unless someone is motivated to make them happen. Something may be a very good idea but it does not happen unless someone is given the responsibility of making it happen.

In business everyone knows that 'creativity' is a good idea and essential when information, technology and competence have all become commodities. While everyone pays lip-service to creativity, nothing much really happens until there is a 'nominated champion' whose business it is to see that creativity becomes an active part of the corporate culture.

It is the same with simplicity. Most people are in favour of simplicity (not all, as we shall see later). But nothing much is going to happen unless someone is given the responsibility for making it happen.

There will always be talented designers and law-makers who strive for simplicity. They can do this in their own work, but this does not affect the work of others.

So there is a need for a formal body whose sole and direct business it is to focus on simplicity. There would be cooperation and liaisons with all sorts of other bodies.

Once a game is laid out in a clear manner, people become very good at playing that game. The game of simplicity needs to be as clearly defined as was the game of quality.

The role of the Institute for Simplicity

1. One role of the institute would be to pass judgement on new laws, regulations, procedures, etc. The institute would examine these things and then declare them to be: acceptable, complex, too complex or much too complex. There could even be a star rating system where five stars was an achievement in complexity. This judgement would be exercised in a number of possible ways: a panel of experts, a random jury, focus groups as in consumer research, opinion polls, etc. The judgement would have no legal force but would make clear that some 'formal' body had expressed a strong opinion. This would be enough.

2. The institute would set up task forces to try to find simpler ways of doing things which seemed too complex. This would be done in co-operation with other bodies. The institute would provide the catalyst and the driving force but the main work would be done by people in their own field.

3. The institute would have a research and education function. There would be a need to develop methods for training people in simplicity and encouraging an element of simplicity in operation and design.

4. There would be a monitoring body to make sure the institute itself did not become too complex.

Getting involved in trying to make things more simple is good for you and good for society. It is almost as important as ecology.

Simplicity should become a permanent fashion.

Suggestion 2

There could be a National Simplicity Campaign in every country

Practical details on how such a National Simplicity Campaign could be organized are given in the Appendix (*see* page 289). This could be done through a national newspaper, local newspapers, local radio stations, etc. All that is required is the will to do it and some organizing ability.

Members of the public would be invited to send in suggestions of two sorts:

1. Areas, matters and procedures which seem unnecessarily complex and which demand simplification. It is enough to identify such areas. There is no need to offer simplifying suggestions.

2. Specific suggestions as to how certain things could be made simpler. There is a need to keep practicality, cost and acceptance in mind.

Suggestions could be published locally and awards might be given.

The campaign could be a yearly event. Such a campaign would act in parallel to the Institute for Simplicity in keeping attention on the need for simplicity.

Almost everyone sees a value in simplicity. Why?

Chapter 1

What Use Is Simplicity?

What Is the Value of Simplicity?

Why Do We Need Simplicity?

Why Is Simple Better?

Dealing with complexity
is an inefficient and
unnecessary waste of
time, attention and
mental energy.

There is never any
justification for things
being complex when they
could be simple.

Simplicity makes life simpler

That heading says nothing – except that we almost automatically equate 'simpler' with 'easier'. One of the main purposes of simplicity is indeed to make life easier.

From complexity come stress, anxiety and frustration. There are few things more annoying and frustrating than dealing with a piece of machinery (electronic or other) which will not do what it is supposed to do. The instructions are invariably too complex and the point you really need is hidden deep inside some subsection somewhere – and the index is always inadequate. The first line in any instruction book should be 'What to do when things freeze up'.

I have often suggested that computers should have a prominent yellow key marked with an S. This is the 'simple' key. When you press it the computer goes into 'simple mode'. This can either be pre-set and standard or programmed to your special preferences.

———

Learning things backwards is usually much simpler than learning them forwards. If you have to learn a sequence of A B C D you would usually learn A first and then B and then C and then D. This means that you are always moving from an area you know very well to an area you do not know. The chances of making a diversion or a mistake are very high. Much learning time is spent unlearning mistakes.

When you learn backwards, you learn D first and then C and then B and finally A. In this way you are always moving forward into an area you already know. Over the ages choir masters have often used this method. It is much more effective – but rarely used in education as educators do not always use the best methods of teaching. At first learning things backwards may seem more complex but in practice it turns out to be easier and simpler. While this

The human brain tries its hardest to simplify life by setting up routine patterns of perception and of action. Once you identify the pattern you flow along it without further effort.

applies to straightforward sequences it is not so easy to apply it to concept levels.

———————

The USA may be the only country in the world where there is no passport control on leaving the country. As I have stood in long queues awaiting a very detailed passport check, I have often wondered what the USA is missing out on. What do countries with elaborate departure passport checks gain that the USA is losing? I suspect that the gain is very small compared to the cost and inconvenience.

Leaving India is rather a complex process. You have to pay a departure tax in local currency, then you have passport control and then you need to get a customs stamp. Why?

In many cases it seems that procedures that were established many years ago, possibly for very good reasons, continue because no one has thought of changing them.

In the Schengen group of countries in Europe it is now possible to pass from one country to another without any passport control at all. This is a great improvement in simplification.

———————

The real purpose of thinking is to abolish thinking. As a self-organizing information system, the human brain allows incoming information to organize itself into routine patterns. (*See* my book *The Mechanism of Mind*.) These patterns form the basis of perception. So when we look at something we instantly recognize it instead of having to work it out every time.

The same applies to action. With eleven pieces of clothing to put

There is always the possibility that there is a simpler way to do something. Even if that is not always the case it is always worth investing some thinking time and creative effort in trying to find a simpler approach.

on when you get up in the morning there are 39,916,800 possible ways of getting dressed. There are eleven choices for the first piece, ten for the next – and so on. Life would be very slow and complex if you had to figure it out every morning. So routines simplify life both as regards perception and also as regards action.

It is true that we can get trapped in routines and need creative thinking to get us out of the trap, but routines do have a value in simplying life.

Simplicity makes it much easier to do things

Often the traditional way of doing things is long and complex. A simpler way can sometimes be found.

There are 131 entrants for a singles elimination tennis tournament. How many matches do there have to be in order to produce the champion?

It is possible to work this out in the traditional way by working backwards. There is to be one match in the finals. There will be two matches in the semifinals – and so on. Eventually you will come to the first round. Some players will have byes and go straight into the second round.

There is a simpler way to do it.

If there is one winner then there must be 130 losers in the tournament. Since each loser is produced by one match there needs to be 130 matches to produce 130 losers. It is as simple as that.

———

It would be unfair to suggest that there is always a simpler way of

An expert is someone
who has succeeded in
making decisions and
judgements simpler
through knowing what
to pay attention to and
what to ignore.

doing things. There is always the 'possibility' of a simpler way. At times there may be no simpler way, or it may be very hard to find.

Finding a simpler way is usually neither simple nor easy.

It could be argued, with validity, that it would be best always to use the same traditional routine instead of looking for a simpler way, which might not be there. Such a standard approach might be 'simpler' from the operations point of view. I would not strongly disagree with that. Sometimes, however, the simpler way is so strikingly simple that it may be worth investing some time and effort in finding a simpler way.

———————

Experts progressively make life easier for themselves by simplifying their judgements and decisions. Over time they learn which are the important things to look for. From a mass of data they learn to pick out what really matters. They learn the key discriminators which decide between one situation and another. They learn to ignore the less reliable discriminators, which work only part of the time. An expert doctor learns to focus on the key sign or symptom.

A neural network computer can be trained to do the same thing. Over time it learns to rely on certain features and to rely less on other features.

———————

Design for manufacture means paying attention to making things simpler to produce. Some of the results of this relatively simple attitude are spectacular. One car manufacturer used to assemble a sun-roof from sixty different parts. It is now put together from just three sub-assemblies.

Things evolve to become ever more complex – not more simple.

Those who have got used to the complexity no longer notice it and even add more elements, so increasing the complexity even further.

Production engineers are usually skilled enough to cope with complexity and often no longer notice it. A deliberate design towards simplicity can make things much easier.

There is no natural evolution towards simplicity. In practice things get ever more complex rather than simpler. This happens because additional functions and features are always being added. It is not always feasible to go back and to start from scratch each time a new feature has to be added. This applies particularly in the legal world where a stream of qualifications and amendments is added to the current base. It is not practical to redesign at every step. Even if it were practical there is little motivation to do so.

Some people get so used to the complexity of the existing system that they no longer regard it as complex. So they simply add further bits and pieces in a higgledy-piggledy manner.

It is said, possibly unfairly, that London taxi-cabs have to be high enough to allow passengers to wear top hats, and that they are also required to carry a bundle of hay for the horse. Usually there is no inbuilt mechanism to kill laws when they have outlasted their usefulness. Perhaps every law should be allocated a lifespan at birth.

From time to time a genuine effort is made to simplify forms. But the process is difficult if it is only undertaken by people who know the system. They cannot see why anyone should find ambiguities or difficulties. Perhaps there could be a professional 'simple-minded' body which could be hired to 'misunderstand' basic instructions. The experts would then have to outwit the simple-minded people so that these people could no longer make mistakes.

It may be better to simplify a process rather than train people to cope with the complexity.

It was a very long time before USA immigration forms accepted the fact that most of the rest of the world (who would be using such forms) indicated the date as day / month / year rather than the month / day / year as used in the USA. Surely it would be easier to train the few people examining the forms than to hope to train the millions visiting the USA. This matter has now been put right.

From this example comes the important point: for whose convenience are forms designed? Are they designed for the convenience of those reading the forms and acting upon the forms? Or are forms designed for ease of understanding and ease of co-operation from those filling in the forms? The two are very rarely the same thing. Perhaps forms should get a seal of approval from the Institute for Simplicity.

Some operations require skilled workers. Sometimes this is because the operation has evolved over time and become ever more complex. Skilled workers are hard to find and expensive to employ. If you cannot find skilled workers in the market then you have to train your own workers. Many processes could be made much easier through a deliberate attempt to simplify the process.

Whose business is it to simplify processes? This could come under 'quality' or 're-engineering' or 'design for manufacture'. It would probably be more effective if there was a deliberate attempt to simplify things.

When I was doing a lot of work with Du Pont in teaching creative thinking methods, they told me how the application of creativity had reduced the number of moving parts at one point in a process by 80 per cent.

Reviewing and re-examining procedures, processes and matters

Once simplicity is set as a key value we can make improvements in that direction.

People find thinking to be difficult because civilization has never made any attempt to make thinking simpler.

Outside technical areas, perception is far more important than logic. But we have persisted in focusing on logic.

which are not problems can result in serious simplification. Far too often we use thinking just for problem solving and putting right defects.

The major use for thinking is not in problem solving but in improving what we are doing and finding new things to do (value creation).

Once we come to regard simplicity as a value then we can start to improve in the direction of 'simplicity'.

Thinking is a complex process because we have never made any attempt to make it a simpler process. We have tied ourselves up in complex rules of logic and philosophical qualifications when most practical thinking takes place in 'perception'. I have always found that most of the mistakes in thinking are not mistakes of logic at all but mistakes of perception. David Perkins at Harvard tells me that his research supports this view and that up to 90 per cent of the mistakes in thinking are indeed mistakes of perception.

Once we have understood how perception is based on the behaviour of the neural networks of the brain as a self-organizing information system, then we can design extremely simple tools for thinking. These tools are so very simple that they are used by four-year-olds in school (Clayfield College, Brisbane) and top executives of some of the world's largest corporations such as Siemens (the largest corporation in Europe).

An explorer returns from a newly discovered island. The explorer reports that he noticed a smoking volcano and a strange bird which could not fly. What else was there? The explorer says that he only noticed the volcano and the bird. That was all that 'caught his attention'. So you send the explorer back and give him a simple 'attention-directing' framework. Look north and note down what

For the first time workers have been provided with very simple thinking tools which allow them to take charge of their work and their lives.

Thinking is not only concerned with contemplative philosophy but also with doing in the real world.

you see. Then look east and note down what you see. Then south and west. The explorer can now direct his attention at will instead of waiting for it to be 'caught' by something interesting.

The CoRT (Cognitive Research Trust) thinking lessons have now been in use in various schools around the world for twenty-five years. They are so simple that some academics get very upset by their simplicity. Susan Mackie, a brilliant teacher, has been teaching some of these tools at the bottom of a platinum mine in South Africa to illiterate miners who speak up to fourteen different mother tongues. There could be few educational situations more disadvantaged.

The effect on the workers has been extraordinary. For the first time in their lives they now have some simple thinking tools for taking charge of their lives. Productivity has gone up, absenteeism is down and safety performance is up. Workers now go home and made budgets for the first time ever. One man reported how he had taught the very simple tools to his three wives and had had peace at home for the last three months. Another man recounted how his larger wife had ceased beating him once she had learned the thinking tools. A quarrel between two of the underground locomotive drivers was instantly sorted out when both used the simple tool OPV (other people's views). A group of these miners trained in simple thinking methods put forward safety suggestions that were so good they are being considered by the National Safety Council.

In Ireland, John O'Sullivan, the chief executive of the ALPS company, started teaching thinking skills to the work-force. Through their suggestions they saved so much money for the company that he can now pay the 'thinkers' extra wages. Working through Barry Lynch, the shop floor became so well trained that a group of them designed a new computer keyboard, which is now in production.

Again in South Africa, Susan Mackie was teaching in a very poor

Complexity means distracted effort. Simplicity means focused effort.

school in a disadvantaged area. She divided the class into halves. One half were taught just four of the CoRT tools; the other half were not. Each pupil brought to school 5 rand (about 150 US cents at the time). By the end of the year the group using the very simple thinking tools had made a profit of R45,000. The other group had made R10,000.

In Australia youths who cannot find a job are sometimes brought together as a 'job club', for which someone takes responsibility. The usual success rate is 40 per cent employment. Jennifer Sullivan had charge of two 'job clubs'. All the young members of the clubs were deaf. In one club she obtained 100 per cent employment (sustained). In the other job club she got 70 per cent employment. The difference was that she taught them some of the basic CoRT thinking tools.

So some very simple 'attention-directing' thinking tools make life easier and simpler. Thinking does not have to be complicated. So very simple are these thinking tools that one Canadian academic declared, in print, that the tools could not possibly work because, on philosophical grounds, they were too simple. That is like saying that, on philosophical grounds, cheese does not exist. But it does. That is too often the difference between academic theorizing and real-life application. Simplicity does work and can be very powerful.

Simple systems are easier to set up, easier to monitor and easier to repair

Simpler systems are usually easier to operate. This seems obvious and there may be some doubt as to why I used the term 'usually'. Surely simple systems are 'always' easier to operate – by definition? It rather depends on the reference point for the simplicity. Usually simplicity does refer to people. But it may refer mainly to the system itself. It is possible to have a system which is simple in itself (few

Simplicity with respect to what? The reference point could be the system in itself, or the user of the system.

relationships, few moving parts, etc.) which might just be more complex to operate.

Simple systems are easier to set up. Even this is not absolute. For example, a system which has to be adjusted to be accurate may be simpler in itself than one which has a self-adjusting mechanism, but may be more complex to set up because of the need for accurate adjustment. A self-focusing camera is simpler to use than a manually focused camera but is a more complex mechanism in itself.

So there are two points to make here.

1. Simplicity has to have a reference point: simple with reference to what? The usual reference points are: the system in itself; the system in terms of the user.

2. Comments made in this book are not made in the usual philosophical sense of 'always' and 'never' but in the sense of 'usually' and 'by and large'. So you may well find special exceptions to the comments I make – but the comments still apply 'by and large'. Socrates used to spend his whole time finding rare and special exceptions to anything anyone said. He must have been most irritating.

─────────

When a complex system goes wrong it is usually hard to tell exactly what has happened. The failure may be at several places. When a car breaks down the average motorist finds it hard to tell what has happened. When a doctor is faced with a breakdown in the complex system of the human body, it is not always easy to tell what has happened. In a simple system there are fewer points to check and fewer interactions to examine.

There is the modular approach to simplicity. In setting things up a few standard modules are coupled together. Different standard modules may be put together to give a variety of products. At one

Breaking things down into smaller units, decentralization and modular design are all approaches to simplicity – so long as the unity of the overall purpose is not lost.

Simplicity very often involves the 'trading-off' of one value against another.

point General Motors was alleged to be doing this with its car production. Customized computers work on the same basis. You phone up Dell and tell them exactly what you want in your personal computer. If the modules are standard, then you get what you requested.

The modular approach makes diagnosis and repair easier. You check each module and repair the one that is faulty. Doctors would love to be able to do this with the human body: organ transplant is an approach. Modularization, chunking and creating units is one of the basic approaches to simplification – but it can be overdone.

When every decision and every order has to come from a central command and filter down through other layers of command, the system becomes complex. When local leaders have the ability to make their own decisions within clearly defined frameworks and with clearly defined general objectives, then the system is simpler and more responsive. The emphasis has to be on the 'defined' framework. If this is not clearly in place then every local decision maker makes different decisions and the result is a complex chaos which is very difficult to monitor.

As will become apparent throughout this book, simplicity is often a matter of 'trade-off'. You gain simplicity in one respect but you may increase the risk in another respect.

A machine is simple and predictable in its behaviour. But it has to be adjusted to suit differing conditions. A self-adjusting machine with electronic feedback and computer control is much more complex in itself but does its own adjustment.

Simple procedures save time, money and energy

Once again this statement is not absolute.

Centrelink is a bold
attempt by the Australian
government to simplify
life for the users of the
various welfare agencies.
It may also simplify
administration.

On toll roads cars have to stop and pay a toll. There is usually a need for people to operate the tolls as motorists rarely have the right change to pay an automatic toll. There are now systems where the driver does not stop at all. A reader on the side of the road records an electronic tag on the car. Eventually a bill is sent to the motorist. Such a system results in much simpler traffic flow and ease of operation. It may be more expensive to set up but a lot of wage costs are saved in reducing the manning of toll booths. At the same time the cost of billing and receiving payment must also be taken into account. The system does save journey time.

In the same way electronic tickets at airports save time and energy and people costs.

The Australian government is trying a bold experiment. All the welfare agencies are now grouped together: unemployment, study grants, child benefits, pensions, etc. This means that instead of a person having to go from agency to agency all over town, there is now a 'one-stop' place where everything is dealt with. This is certainly very much simpler from the user's point of view. It may also simplify administration and building costs. This is a bold attempt at a much-needed simplification of systems which are universally complex and designed (or have evolved) more from the point of view of the provider than that of the receiver. Far too often the attitude is: 'Be grateful that you are getting a grant – don't expect us to make it too easy for you.'

A business has control over its market. The business can choose to expand or not expand. A retail chain can choose to open a shop in this city but not in that city. If a store runs out of supplies that is their business. In contrast, the public service has its market determined for it by the legislators. There is a need to cope, instantly and universally, with what has been determined by the legislators.

There is an aesthetic
appeal to simplicity both
in art and, even more, in
science.

Discovering the under-
lying simplicity of a
process is far more likely to
be useful than imaginative
and complex description
of phenomena.

Customers also have the 'right' to demand service. So it is very easy to be critical of the apparent inefficiencies of public-sector bureaucracy. Nowhere else is there a greater need for a permanent simplification campaign.

I have sometimes suggested that if a public servant could genuinely abolish his or her own job that person should continue to receive the full salary. The cost is no greater than if the person was still at work – and now there is a saving in all the support costs. That able person would also be released to take – and then abolish – a second job and so get two salaries. Such an idea makes economic sense but would never be acceptable. (Of course, the job would have to be genuinely abolished and not just dumped on someone else.)

The motivation for simplification is often poor because people are asked to find ways to abolish their own jobs (cut their own throats).

Simplicity is elegant

There is an aesthetic appeal to simplicity. This may be in terms of architecture, clothes or scientific theory. Scientists are always looking for simple theories that explain a lot of things. In a sense the whole of science has been based on this search for simplicity. Before modern science all happenings were explained as the complex interaction of different spirits, gods, hobgoblins, etc. You only have to look at the Greek pantheon or Hindu cosmology to see how complex explanations could become. There is no limit to the complexity of description. Psychoanalysis is a more modern example. The aim of science was to move from unfettered imaginative description to the seeking out of the simple underlying mechanisms.

The human brain is a very simple system that is capable of working in a complex way, rather than a complex system.

Outside of art, complexity
for the sake of complexity
has no value whatsoever.

Complexity is always
failed simplicity.

The simplicity and elegance of Greek architecture, Georgian architecture and the Bauhaus movement all illustrate the attraction of elegant simplicity. The same applies to writing and to poetry. The simple and elegant metaphor can be more powerful than the most purple prose.

At the same time, there is also the attraction of the richness of Gothic and Baroque architecture. It is not a matter of mutual exclusion. In aesthetics there can be the appeal of the simple and the elegant and at the same time the appeal of the rich and intricate. If you like fish it does not mean that you cannot like beef. If you like Bach it does not mean you cannot also like Peter Gabriel.

Outside the field of aesthetics, complexity for the sake of complexity has no value whatsoever. There are times when complexity is necessary because we have not yet found a simpler way to do something. But we do not treasure the complexity as such. We may want complex functions and behaviour, but we would still like to deliver these in as simple a way as possible. A restaurant might like to provide you with a wide range of dishes, but it would still like to simplify its ordering, cooking and delivery.

There are those who value a simple life-style and there are others who enjoy variety and richness – but they would still like to avoid hassle, complications and frustrations.

Simplicity is powerful

Simplicity is powerful in all the meanings and applications of that word. This is because simplicity is a unification around a purpose.

Simplicity is not natural.
You have to choose to
make it happen.

To get simplicity you
have to want it badly
enough.

Chapter 2

The Challenge of Simplicity

The Search for Simplicity

The Effort to Simplify

The Urge to Simplify

Investing in Simplicity

The challenge was to invent a real game where each player had only one playing piece.

The first rule of simplicity is that you must want to simplify

Occasionally, simplicity might just happen. There are certain people who are so fond of simplicity that anything they do tends to be simple. On the whole simplicity does not happen by chance. You have to want to make something simple. There has to be a drive, an urge, a motivation to make things simpler.

———

Many years ago I was having dinner at the high table in Trinity College, Cambridge. I was sitting next to Professor Littlewood, who was an outstanding and justly famous mathematician. At one point we were discussing the matter of getting computers to play chess. We agreed that chess was not a very sophisticated game. This is because chess achieves difficulty through complexity. There are many pieces and different moves. It is not hard to get difficulty through complexity. Sophistication depends on getting difficulty through 'simplicity'. So as a self-imposed challenge, I said I would invent a real game in which each player has only one playing piece.

I went away and invented the L-game which can be learned in about twenty seconds. It is played on a simple four-by-four board. Each player has an L-shaped piece which can be placed in any position at each turn so long as it does not cover exactly the same squares as before. In addition there are two small neutral pieces that cover just one square and do not belong to either player. After moving the L-piece a player may (optional) move either neutral piece to any new position. It is as simple as that.

The purpose of the game is to block the opponent so that there is no place to which the opponent can move his or her L-piece.

In this game you cannot win by winning. You can only win if your opponent does well.

Cartoonists constantly face the challenge of simplicity. How can a complex concept be expressed simply?

There are over 18,000 possible moves. The game has been analysed several times on computers and there is no one winning strategy which the first player could use to ensure victory.

A short time ago the US producer of the game (Mark Chester) asked me to design a new game which could accompany the L-game in order to give a twin product package. As a challenge I set out to design the first 'social justice game'. It ended up by being even simpler than the L-game and is played on a three-by-three board (as for noughts and crosses or tic tac toe). It is a social justice game because you cannot win by winning. If you try too hard to win you lose.

Contact: Mark Chester, Rex Games (USA)
Tel: 1 415 777 2900 or 1 800 542 6375
Fax: 1 415 777 1013
Web site: http://www.rexgames.com

Cartoonists are always facing the challenge to simplify. In one small frame and often with stock characters, they have to convey what can be complex concepts. This is creative simplicity at its best. I am an admirer of the skill of cartoonists. A writer can string together sentences to amble around a subject and, sometimes, make sense. A cartoonist cannot do that. The cartoon must be crisp, clear, simple and amusing. For a cartoon to work it has to be simple in concept even if the drawing is more elaborate. There are times when a cartoon works at several levels. But at each level it has to be simple and clear.

There are times when complexity in a machine allows greater simplicity of operation.

Today computers allow us to do some things in a much simpler way than ever before.

An advertising copywriter faces three challenges: finding a simple message; finding a theme that is rich and evocative; and finding a simple way to express the message. It is the combination of richness and simplicity which is unusual. The famous Avis slogan 'We try harder' was very simply expressed but rich in meaning: we try to please you; we are not complacent; we are continually improving; we are at your service, etc. The challenge is not that different from the challenge facing a cartoonist.

Software designers continually face the challenge of simplicity. Doing it the complex way may require dozens of lines of code. The simple way may only require half a dozen lines. Does it matter? The quicker approach is easier to put down, is easier to check and uses less disc space. Today's computers have so much capacity that it probably does not matter that much if the software is unnecessarily lengthy. The main point is that it should be easier to debug or alter.

Because computers are so fast and powerful it is sometimes possible to be simple in a complex way. For example, there are various formulae which can calculate the flow of water around the hull of a ship (or air over a plane wing). With a computer it can be done as an 'iterative process'. This means working out a model in which each element of water (or air) interacts with another. This process is gone over again and again to give a final result that is more accurate than the formula approach. The paradox is that the interactive approach is much more tedious and time-consuming even though it is basically a simple approach. The computer does all the work and so makes it simple to use a simple approach that without a computer would have been far too complex.

The main aim of com-
munication is clarity and
simplicity. Usually they
go together – but not
always.

Communication is always
understood in the context
and experience of the
receiver – no matter what
was intended.

In writing and in giving lectures and seminars there is often a need to communicate complex matters in a simple way. Suppose you wanted to illustrate some of the aspects of change.

You start with the letter 'a' and then you add another letter. At each point the combined letters must form a recognized word. So the sequence might go:

a
at
cat
coat
actor
factor
factory

In some cases there is a simple addition. At another point there may be an insertion. Occasionally there is a need for total restructuring, as in the change from 'coat' to 'actor'.

This is a simple way of showing how change may simply be an addition but sometimes needs to be a fundamental restructuring. I once set this as an exercise on my web site (http://edwdebono. com/) and some contributors had sequences over twelve stages long.

In any communication there is a fundamental challenge to simplicity. How can this be expressed simply and clearly? Complexity can lead to confusion. At the same time (as with instructions) you do have to imagine the ambiguities and misunderstandings that might arise. You have to seek to prevent these. Too simple a message may be elegant but might be open to misinterpretation. When you set out to write rules for a game you will be surprised to find that

Because simplicity seems
easy we believe it is easy
to achieve. When it is not
easy to achieve we give
up too quickly.

a rule which seems perfectly clear to you can easily be misunderstood even by very intelligent players. The reason is that players are very rarely starting from scratch. There are other games they play and other habits they have. They may therefore interpret your rules on another basis. For example, the rule in the L-game that a player simply moves the piece to a new position can be misinterpreted in at least two ways:

1. Some players believe the piece can only be slid into a new position, whereas it can be lifted up, turned over and put down anywhere a player likes.

2. Some players believe that a 'new position' means a new placing for the entire L-piece. It is enough that one of the squares covered by the L-piece in its new position is different from the squares covered in the preceding position.

Simplicity is not easy

Any valuable creative idea will always be logical in hindsight – otherwise we would be unable to appreciate the value of the idea. It would remain a crazy idea for ever – or at least until the existing paradigm changed. Because such ideas are 'logical' in hindsight, we have always believed that they could have been reached by logic, with no need for creativity. This has been the prevalent belief and it is totally false. It is based on passive information systems. In self-organizing 'active' information systems asymmetric patterns are formed. This means that the route from A to B may be round-about but the route from B to A is direct. That is the basis of both humour and creativity.

Imagine an ant on the trunk of a tree. What is the chance of that ant getting to one specified leaf? At every branch point the chances diminish. In an average tree the chances of an ant getting to one

We are usually too ready
to accept the first solution
as good enough. We need
to believe that there is
often a better or simpler
solution in order to keep
on thinking.

specified leaf are about one in eight thousand – not very high. Now imagine the ant sitting on a leaf. What are the chances of that ant getting to the trunk of the tree? One in one, or 100 per cent. From the trunk to the leaf there are many branches and possible routes. From the leaf to the trunk there are no branches.

It is the same with both creativity and simplicity. Once a creative or simple solution has been achieved it seems very easy and simple in hindsight.

The danger is that people come to believe that simplicity is easy. When they fail to achieve simplicity they believe that simplicity is not possible in that particular situation.

Simplicity will not happen unless people are prepared to work hard at simplicity and make a real effort to achieve it.

Too easily satisfied

When we find a solution to a problem we are so delighted that we never stop to consider that there might be a 'better' or 'simpler' solution. We have found an 'answer' and that should be enough. We move on to the next problem. This may be human nature or it may be a hangover from schooldays, when there was one right answer and if you got that answer you had succeeded. Real life is, unfortunately, rather more complex than the problems set in school books. It may not be too difficult to find a way – even a standard way – of doing something and then to find a much better way. There is a traditional saying that 'the good is the enemy of the best'. It simply means that if we have something which is 'good enough' or 'adequate', we rarely make an effort to find something better.

If you come to believe
that simplicity is as real
and as important a value
as cost, then you will
make more effort to
achieve simplicity.

The obvious alternatives
are only some of the
alternatives that can be
found – or designed.

When we are looking at cost, we do sometimes make the effort to find something better than the first solution that comes to mind. If the first solution is rather expensive, then we continue to look for a cheaper solution or way of doing things. Could we get into the habit of making the same effort to find something 'simpler'?

If you really believe that 'simplicity' is as important a direction as 'cost', then you might make that effort. I suspect that very few people do believe this.

When we are looking for alternatives we lay out the obvious alternatives. Too often we believe that these alternatives cover all the possibilities.

How would you weigh a cat?

You could weigh a cardboard box with high sides. Then you put the cat in the box on the scales. You subtract the weight of the box from the total and you have the weight of the cat.

You could drug the cat or wait for it to fall asleep and then gently place it on the scales.

You could arrange some food on an enlarged platform on the scales and then see the change in weight when the cat jumped on to the platform to eat the food.

It is obvious that there is a way that is simpler than all of these.

You hold the cat in your arms and get on to the scales. You then subtract your weight from the total.

The willingness to look for further alternatives is similar to the

Simplicity is important as a sought-for value.

Simplicity is even more important as a permanent habit of mind – as a style of thinking.

willingness to look for better solutions. There has to be the belief that there might be simpler alternatives (or solutions). There can be no guarantee that there are simpler solutions or alternatives – or that you will be able to find them. It is a matter of being willing to invest time and effort in that search. On any one occasion it might indeed be wasted time. But overall you will find better solutions and better alternatives than if you had been satisfied with the first thing that came to mind.

Would you really like to have been called by the very first name that came to your parents' minds?

Simplicity as a value and as a habit

If something is a value you will take it into account. If simplicity is a defined value then you will make an effort to improve matters in the direction of 'simplicity'. If simplicity is a value then you will appreciate suggestions that make things more simple. If simplicity is an acknowledged value then simplicity becomes part of your judgement screen when you are looking at things or for things. If simplicity is a value then that value can form part of any thinking or discussion.

So, obviously, I am much in favour of simplicity being treated as a real value.

Much more important than simplicity as a value is simplicity as a habit. This means that simplicity becomes an automatic part of the design process whenever thinking is used. Values can be ignored but habits cannot be ignored.

If simplicity has such a high value, how is it that there seem to be some people who do not like simplicity?

Chapter 3

Why Some People Love Complexity

Why Some People Hate Simplicity

Why Some People Get Very Upset by Simplicity

Simplistic

Over-Simplification

Why You Have to Know Your Subject Very Well to Be Simple

There are some very practical reasons why a few people delight in complexity and hate, hate simplicity.

Complexity has its value?

If you want to be taken very very seriously then write a very very complex book – in French, if possible. Several things then happen.

1. If you really have nothing to say, it is better to make it as complex as possible otherwise people will see that nothing is being said.

2. Critics will love the book because they will feel specifically privileged that only they can understand it.

3. Critics will find that there is a lot to write about the book – which is never the case with a simple book.

4. Academics will love the book because obviously the book needs the special skill of the academic for its interpretation to ordinary people.

5. No one will dare criticize the book because they are never quite sure that they have understood it.

6. Any philosopher is free to read into the book anything he or she wants because the complexity encourages any interpretation.

7. People will buy the book to show their cultural superiority but will not actually read it.

8. A cult will develop around the mystique of the book.

9. It will naturally be assumed that the author is a very profound thinker struggling to express immensely complex thoughts.

10. Any number of self-appointed intellectuals will have a very good time enjoying the complexity.

The easiest way to be 'superior' is to pretend to understand what others cannot understand. For that you need complexity.

Apparently complex matters provide a position for interpreters of that complexity. Simple matters remove that role.

If you think these comments are unfair, just keep them in mind and keep your eyes open. You will find ample evidence to justify them. You will find a mystique and adoration of the complex by those who cannot understand the simple.

The easiest way to be 'superior' is to understand what ordinary people cannot understand. If the matter is simple, how can you show your superiority? The pseudo-understanding of what is really unintelligible is a great game – with many players.

Why some people hate simplicity

It may be that some people really enjoy complexity just as some people enjoy intrigue. It may be that some people really enjoy complexity in the same way that some people really enjoy Gothic or Baroque architecture. The minds of such people are actively engaged by the complexity. Simplicity, on the other hand, is very much harder work. You are required to look below the simplicity. I wonder how many physicists were really upset when Einstein proposed his formula: $E = mc^2$?

Simplicity is hard work if you do not know the subject very well. With simplicity there is nothing to get your teeth into. With complexity there is always some ragged edge somewhere which you can bite on.

As I mentioned above, there is also the underlying fear that the role of the interpreter will no longer be necessary if the matter is simple enough for ordinary people to understand and use. Academics feel a great insecurity about this.

Simplicity before under-
standing is simplistic;
simplicity after under-
standing is simple.

There is also a strong feeling of 'unfairness'. If you have struggled with the complexity of a subject, why should that subject be made simple for other people? This is unfair.

———————

There is a strong element of jealousy too. If someone has managed to produce something simple there is the basic jealousy: 'Why didn't I think of that?'

Paradoxically, the more intense the hatred and the jealousy, the greater is the real appreciation for what has been made simple. Why be jealous of something which is worthless?

Simplistic

Of course, everyone would claim that the real justification for hating simplicity is that it is not simplicity at all but 'simplistic'.

It is perfectly true that there can be 'simplistic' approaches to a matter by someone who does not understand the matter fully. If a government does not have enough money, why don't they just print more money? That is a simplistic approach which has led to hyper-inflation in many South American economies in the past. This practice was only brought to an end by a fuller understanding of monetarism.

'If you give everyone more money they will be happy.' This is a fairly simplistic approach to human nature.

In the past, when science was less developed, all phenomena were due to the direct action of some god or spirit. When crops grew or when crops failed there was some sort of 'personal' action on the part of the god or spirit. These beings had to be placated with

Oversimplification means carrying simplification to the point where other values are ignored.

sacrifices of food and other offerings. Although very useful as a belief framework, such explanations might have been regarded as simplistic.

'Simplistic' often means jumping from an observed phenomenon to a direct and simple explanation, missing out all the true complexity of the situation.

It is somewhat simplistic to believe that putting sanctions on a country will really cause the leaders of that country to change their behaviour. Yet the UN Security Council does this all the time – probably because there is nothing else to do.

Oversimplification

Oversimplification is not quite the same as 'simplistic'. Simplistic means that you do not understand the subject and so come up with a simplistic approach. Oversimplification means that you have simplified the matter too much and have left out important aspects of it. The oversimplification is not wrong, but it is inadequate because it is incomplete. Many economists believe that the 'monetarism' mentioned earlier is an 'oversimplification' of the dynamics of inflation. In practice it does work – but at the cost of an inhibition of growth.

Oversimplification is simplification carried too far. There are those who believe that some modern architecture has gone too far in its drive for elegant simplicity.

When does the process of simplification have to stop?

When I am lecturing I draw the whole time on an overhead projector. It would take far too long to draw complete human figures so I draw simple 'stick figures'. Why not simplify matters

In order to make some-
thing simple you have to
know your subject very
well indeed.

even more by just drawing short vertical lines to represent people? Because such lines would not easily be identified as people. The gain in simplicity has resulted in a loss of communication clarity.

Simplification stops when the values derived from simplification are balanced out by the increasing loss of other values. Oversimplification means pursuing simplification without paying attention to the loss of other values. You can simplify a sauce so that it is simpler to make but you may have thrown out all the flavours.

While oversimplification is a real danger, the term is much too easily and too often used by those who do not like simplicity for all the reasons outlined earlier in this chapter. It is a very easy accusation to make. It also suggests that the person making the accusation has a more profound knowledge of the subject – which is often not the case. It is those who do not know the subject well that insist on complexity.

The big dilemma

In order to make something simple you need to know your subject very well indeed. The following is a quote from one of the three Nobel prize laureates who wrote forewords to my book, *I am Right, You are Wrong*:

At first glance the writing may appear somewhat simplistic because of his style, but upon reflection it is very deep and perceptive. Complex matters can indeed be explained in simple terms if the expositor has a thorough understanding of the subject. De Bono is a master in this art, and he describes in clear terms how and why humans think.

Ivan Giaever

A method which was dismissed as trivial and worthless by one critic has proved very powerful and effective in action because it provides an alternative to the primitive argument system.

Some of the practical techniques of lateral thinking (like the random entry technique) are amazingly simple. Psychologists and philosophers looking at them protest that they cannot possibly work. But in practice they do work. Thousands of ideas can be deliberately generated using such methods. What the protesters never realize is that the techniques are based on a consideration of how the nerve networks in the human brain function as a 'self-organizing' information system. In such systems we now know that there is a mathematical necessity both for provocation and also for random entry. Most of the critics and protesters simply have no idea at all about such matters.

When my book *Six Thinking Hats* was published, a review in the *International Business Digest* by a well-known consultant dismissed it as trivial. The Six Hats method is now in use all round the world in major corporations (ABB, Siemens, BT, Du Pont, Texas Instruments, Federal Express, Motorola, Singapore Public Service, Malaysian Public Service, etc., etc.) and in thousands of schools. The system shortens meeting times to about one quarter of what they would have been. Meetings are more constructive. Ego positions and arguments are excluded. In one meeting of a medical charity in Australia the introduction of the method was so successful that a director asked for it to be put on record that it was the most constructive meeting in fifteen years. So we see that a method which was dismissed as trivial and worthless is actually very useful in practice.

———————

It is quite impossible to distinguish between true simplicity and simplistic unless you yourself know the subject very well. Otherwise your judgement may demonstrate your ignorance.

So the big dilemma is this:

How do you distinguish between what is really simplistic and what is simplicity based on a thorough knowledge of the subject?

The very uncomfortable answer is that you cannot unless you also know the subject very well. There is no way of distinguishing between simplistic and powerful simplicity unless you know the subject – or have watched the processes in action.

So someone who dismisses something as 'being too simple' may simply be demonstrating his or her ignorance of the subject. Critics do it all the time – not realizing how stupid they appear to the many readers who know the subject better than they do.

I am always getting letters from readers commenting on the stupidity of critics who pontificate on matters about which they know very little.

But how do you know that you know very little? That is the other part of the big dilemma.

Why shouldn't language be living and changing all the time?

Chapter 4

Simplifying Simplify and Simplification

A New Suggestion

Language is often cumbersome and inadequate. There is sometimes a need to develop new words or to alter existing words.

A provocative but simplifying suggestion

I am well aware that the suggestion I am about to make in this chapter will irritate some people and much upset others. A few might even be outraged. Others may find the suggestion useful.

There are those who believe that language should never change and that any change is, by definition, a corruption or deterioration of language.

The term 'lateral thinking', which I introduced many years ago, is now a normal part of the English language and is used in print, in television shows and in conversation. That introduction was not too difficult because there was an obvious need for a term to describe a type of thinking that was more concerned with changing starting perceptions and concepts than with working with the traditional ones. Being the conjunction of an adjective with a noun also made the introduction easier.

Another new word I invented was 'po'. There is a real need for this word in language in order to describe something that cannot otherwise be described. 'Po' indicates that something is put forward directly as a provocation. The speaker knows it to be unreasonable and contrary to experience and the speaker knows that the listener knows the speaker knows. A provocation is not for judgement but for 'movement'. We move forward from the provocation to new ideas. There is a mathematical need for provocation in any self-organizing information system like the human brain. Language is all about describing 'what is' and has not developed a signal to indicate a provocation. The nearest we come is 'suppose' or 'what if', but these are still within the range of the possible. Provocation is not.

———

The words around
'simple' are very
cumbersome. What about
simpler words?

simplification = simping

simple = simp

simplicity = simp

simpler = more simp

The word 'simple' is probably simple enough. But words like 'simplify' and 'simplification' are a bit of a mouthful and contradict the simplicity of what they are supposed to be about.

So the provocative suggestion is that we reduce all variations to the simple term 'simp'.

Simp now becomes an adjective: 'This is very simp.'

Simp also becomes a verb: 'Can you simp this.'

The process of 'simplification' now becomes 'simping': 'There is a need for some simping here.'

The suggestion is very simple. There are two points where there could be a problem.

The first point is the existing word 'simper'. This problem is easily overcome by using 'more simp' and 'most simp'.

The word 'simp' is already in use in a minor way as a colloquial term for 'simpleton'. I happen to think that 'simpleton' is a very rude and abusive term. If it is supposed to mean a 'simple' person then the term is too derogatory, for there is no harm in being simple. If the term is supposed to mean stupid, then I have to say that I have very rarely met a 'stupid' person. The only sort of stupidity I have met is 'arrogance', 'complacency' and 'conceit'. These are the real forms of stupidity. I have found that even the simplest of people can think very well indeed if they are given some basic frames.

I would like to upgrade 'simpleton' to mean someone who sees value in simplicity.

To simplify = to simp

In truth, I would like to upgrade the word 'simpleton' to mean 'someone who sees the value in simplicity'. That may be too outrageous a suggestion, so I shall not make it seriously.

But I do think there is real value in the simplified term 'simp'. I feel we could come to use it easily and naturally. It is not so different from the French pronunciation of 'simple' anyway. I feel it is a good example of 'simping'.

In the rest of this book, I shall use the new term only very occasionally in order to avoid irritating those who will surely be irritated by any suggested change in language.

You need to want to
make things simpler?
Then there are ways to
help you do it.

Intention is the important
step but it can be helped
by method.

Chapter 5

How to Make Things Simpler

How to Simplify

How to 'Simp'

Overview of Methods, Techniques and Approaches

If you are unwilling to be
satisfied with the complex
you will spend more
thinking time trying to
make things simpler.

Almost anything can be
simplified further.

Designing for simplicity

There are at least three possible processes in designing for simplicity.

1. You take something which is already in existence, perhaps has been for years, and you seek to simplify it. You seek to simp the process or procedure. In many areas there is a great need for specific task forces to set about doing this.

2. You are setting out to design something from scratch. There is nothing yet in existence. Can you produce a simple design? How simp is your design going to be?

3. There is a suggested course of action or solution to a problem. This has been accepted and agreed upon. Nevertheless, you are prepared to spend some time making it even simpler.

The first and third processes are very similar. At times the second process may also be similar but with rather more freedom of action.

Simplicity is a value, a habit and an attitude of mind as much as it is a process. If you are not prepared to accept something unless it is simple, then you go on thinking. If you accept something complex because you have no feeling for simplicity, then your outputs will tend to be complex. This simple consideration can determine whether the output is simple or not. You are unlikely to be a good cook unless you have a palate sensitive enough to taste what you have prepared. Your willingness to reject things which are too complex will mean that you spend more thinking time trying to make things simple. You end up putting more energy into simping.

There is a huge overlap between creativity and simplification. There is a need to find alternative and new ways of doing things. This design thinking demands creativity.

Overview of some of the methods

These could be called methods, approaches or techniques. Each of the methods outlined here will be treated in more detail in separate chapters (Chapters 7–11).

As in all 'design' thinking there is a great need for creativity and lateral thinking. Some of the formal methods of lateral thinking will therefore be introduced as appropriate.

1. Historical Review

Many things are there simply because they were there yesterday – and the day before. There may have been a good reason for them at one time but that reason may long since have disappeared. A historical review means looking at the whole operation and also parts of it, and asking 'Is this still necessary?'

2. Shedding, Trimming, Cutting, Slimming, etc.

This is a matter of getting rid of and throwing out everything which cannot justify its presence. This is a sort of 'zero-base' approach where everything has to justify its continued involvement. It is similar to the historical review but much broader.

3. Listening

Listening to people working at the 'sharp end'. They may have useful suggestions as to what is necessary or not necessary. They may have developed valuable short cuts which could never have been derived from theorizing.

4. Combining

Seeking to combine different functions which are currently separate. Trying to 'kill two birds with one stone'.

The ability to extract, define and redesign concepts is the key to the process of simplification.

Sometimes it is much easier to start over again than to try to modify what exists.

5. Extracting Concepts

Here we seek to extract the operating concept behind some action or process and then we seek to find another, simpler, way of delivering that concept.

6. Bulk and Exceptions

Instead of trying to deal with all possible different situations, which is often complex, we separate out the 'bulk' activity and design a simple way to deal with this. Then we make special provisions for the 'exceptions'.

7. Restructuring

This involves a fundamental restructuring of what is being done. This includes such processes as 're-engineering'. This is likely to be more radical than just shedding what is no longer essential.

8. Start Afresh

Go back to the beginning and design from scratch. Ignore the present situation. Design around key values and priorities. Then compare that design to the existing situation.

9. Modules and Smaller Units

Simplify by breaking down the whole situation into smaller units. This may involve modules, 'chunking', decentralization, etc. Each unit is then designed in its own right.

10. Provocative Amputation

Each element or aspect is 'dropped' and then an effort is made to see how the system can be made to work without that element. This is a form of provocation from lateral thinking.

You can build a simpler approach step by step, or you can work downwards from a very broad picture.

Under all the approaches there are three key questions: Why? How? What is the value?

11. Wishful Thinking

Design the ideal 'simple' process and then seek to work from that. If you could have your wish what would the process look like?

12. Shift Energies

Seek to shift the work or the energy from one part of the system to another. For example, shift functions to machines or to other parties.

13. The Ladder Approach

Forget the overall approach. Work incrementally, step by step. At each step consider the value to be delivered by the next step and then the mechanism for delivering that value.

14. The Flavour Approach

This is almost the exact opposite of the ladder approach. Here we take the overall general picture and design to that. Then we seek to make this design practical and concrete.

There is obviously a great deal of overlap between these listed approaches and sometimes they become the same thing. There is a usefulness, however, in keeping them different because there are times when one or other approach proves more effective.

Underlying them all are three key questions:

1. WHY? Why are we doing this at all?

2. HOW? How are we going to carry this out in practice?

3. WHAT IS THE VALUE? Both the positive and negative values. Both for the user of the system and for the system itself.

A metaphor provides a physical model through which we can more easily look at abstract matters.

We can focus attention at different points once we have some model.

Chapter 6

The Tree Metaphor

A Way of Looking at Things

What is the core purpose
of this operation?

What are we really trying
to do here?

Purpose, value and delivery

The tree metaphor is not a method of simplifying things but a way of looking at things. It is therefore not included in the list of methods because it can be part of any of the methods. It is a background metaphor which can help to clarify procedures and even other things.

The trunk of the tree is the basic supporting purpose. What is this all about? Why are we doing this? What do we hope to achieve? What is the intention? What is the core operation?

Sometimes things grow in such a messy fashion that eventually it becomes impossible to tell what the real purpose is. It is said that the purpose of many bureaucracies is to continue in existence. It can happen that something set up for one purpose continues only because its purpose has become that of survival. This is a legitimate enough purpose (everyone seeks to survive) provided other people do not think there should be a different purpose.

In some trees the trunk goes right to the top: as in a fir tree or Christmas tree. The simple branches come off at right angles. In other trees there is a basic trunk which splits into branches and then the branches split again and again. There are many layers of branches. There are even bush-like trees where there is hardly any trunk at all but a lot of branches arising from a short trunk.

We can equate these different sorts of tree to the dominance of the key purpose of the operation. Is that key purpose present at all times or does it tend to get left behind?

Picking out the trunk of the tree is equivalent to identifying the key purpose behind the operation. How dominant is that purpose?

The purpose of any operation is to deliver value to someone.

The best operations deliver value to everyone involved.

There are trees which seem to have several trunks. There are operations which seem to have several purposes. Are these fundamental or are they derived from the main purpose?

The fruit – the values

In the metaphor the fruit at the end of the branches represents the value. The fruit represents food value to birds, animals and humans. For the genes of the tree the fruit represents continuation value.

The purpose of any operation is to deliver value to the users of that operation. To the factory owner the value produced by a machine is represented by the goods produced by that machine. There are the additional values produced by 'quality' and 'freedom from defects' and 'low wastage'. Low power consumption and low maintenance costs for the machine might be further values.

For the people working the machine the values are complex. There is the value of producing a wage through the ultimate sales of the goods produced. There is the value of the machine doing what might have been difficult and tedious to do by hand. There are the additional values of safety, ease of operation and the satisfaction of visible achievement.

At times the values are not at all evenly divided. In the days of slavery, the slaves did not get much of the value beyond that of mere survival.

In any sort of free market or democracy there is much more emphasis on 'delivered value'. Customers are not going to buy something if there is little value. Voters are not going to vote for a government which does not appear to deliver value.

The values are not just the obvious values. There are many less

The less obvious values are sometimes just as important as the more obvious values.

Delivery mechanisms are the link between core intentions and received values.

obvious values. When you buy food the key value is the nutritional value of the food. You need food. But then there are many additional values. There is the taste of the food. There may be a snob value in certain foods. The presentation has a value. The package size has a value. There is the convenience value of being able to walk into a store and buy the food when you like. The storage value of the food is also important. So is the ease of cooking.

The words 'value' and 'benefit' have come to be almost interchangeable for all practical purposes. It could be said that 'value' is the potential that resides in a thing and 'benefit' is the delivery of that value to a person in certain circumstances. Generally speaking the value of gold lies in its preciousness and high price. If you desperately needed a doorstop, then the heavy weight of the gold bar would deliver that benefit to you.

For the sake of simplicity, I shall treat the two words as generally interchangeable.

The branches – the delivery

Between the core purpose (the trunk) and the values (the fruit) there is the delivery system. The delivery system is provided by the branches. The branches provide the mechanism whereby the fruit is made available. The delivery system is made up of the practical, detailed way in which the values are made available.

A shop provides the value of 'convenience'. This convenience is delivered by means of all the concrete details that go into a shop: location, physical building, staff, stocks, delivery, etc., etc.

If you shopped from home via the Internet, then the value of that convenience would be provided by the Internet, by a particular web site and by a shop willing to deliver the ordered goods.

It is usually the delivery mechanisms which need simplifying.

The Centrelink welfare project in Australia is an attempt to simplify the delivery of various welfare payments.

The core purpose of the operation may be general. The values may also be general. But the delivery system has to be practical, detailed and concrete. The delivery system is obviously the most complex of the three elements – just as the branches are the most complicated part of the tree.

So it is hardly surprising that the 'simplification' process is most likely to be applied to the delivery system. At the same time this simplification process will not work unless both the core purpose and the values are kept clearly in mind. There is no point in having a wonderfully simple delivery system which is unable to deliver the values.

Cooking is made up of ways of cooking.

Chapter 7

Three of the Methods of Simping:

– Historical Review

– Shedding

– Listening

Tradition may be a good
reason for continuing to
do something when there
is no other reason. But
you must acknowledge
that reason.

The mystique of wine
may, or may not, affect
the taste and enjoyment
of wine.

Historical review

As well as being one of the finest countries in the world, Australia also produces some of the finest wines in the world. Anyone who does not know about Australian wines does not know much about wine.

Some years ago, in Australia, some tests were done with a screw top for wine bottles instead of the traditional cork. This was the Stelvin cap and it was extremely effective. Blind tastings with wine experts indicated that, on the whole, the wine from bottles with the screw cap were superior to wines from bottles with corks. This is hardly surprising because corks are somewhat unreliable (being a natural product) and the screw cap is totally reliable.

In the market, however, the screw cap failed, for fairly obvious reasons. People associated a screw cap with cheap wines. Also people wanted the grand tradition of pulling the cork out of a bottle. The tradition was part of the whole operation.

If I were trying to introduce the screw cap again, I would put it on some of the most expensive wines. The caps would be made of silver with an enamelled design on the top by a famous artist. The caps would become collectors' items. I would even design a special game to be played with a collection of caps (or they could depict chess pieces).

Wine is difficult to have as a casual drink. If someone asks for a glass of wine you may have to open a new bottle. Unless the whole bottle is consumed, the remainder goes bad through the exposure to air. This seriously restricts the drinking of wine, which tends to be kept for special occasions. In order to overcome this problem, and also in order to make easier the serving of wine at parties, the Australians invented the 'wine cask'. This is a cardboard box inside which is a special plastic bladder which is filled with the wine. The

Although a good idea may be focused in one direction, it must also take all other factors into account.

outlet is a tap on the side of the box. When you want a glass of wine you simply open the tap and fill your glass. Because the plastic bladder decreases in size as the wine is taken from it, there is no contact with air and the wine stays good. It may seem a complicated idea but the purpose is to simplify the drinking of wine both at parties or as a casual drink.

At first, traditionalists in other countries threw up their arms in horror at this sacrilegious treatment of 'sacred' wine. Now the advantages of the 'cask' are being recognized.

Both the above stories (screw cap and cask) are examples of trying to escape from historic procedures. In both cases the new concepts are superior in many respects. But in both cases 'tradition' is itself seen by some as a value. So there is a conflict between change and tradition. (By definition, tradition means no change.)

There is an even simpler way to make wine available as a casual drink. When you buy a bottle of wine decant it with a glass funnel into two, three or four small screw-top bottles. You can now open one or two of the smaller bottles as you wish. Someone could set up a small business selling these small bottles and a glass funnel. That is an example of simplification for a specific purpose: the casual drinking of a single glass of wine.

———————

Men's jackets have buttons on the end of the sleeves. This is a carry-over from the time when sleeves were really 'rolled up'. There is a vent (or two) on the back of a man's jacket. This was from the time when men spent their time riding horses. The vent allowed the bottom of the jacket to spread out when the man was on horseback. Today, not many men ride around during office hours. The buttonhole on one lapel was not really for holding a flower but a means of buttoning up the top of the jacket in cold weather.

If something is not a problem it does not get any thinking time.

A search for simplicity should enable us to rethink everything – not only problem areas.

Jackets today could never be buttoned up in this way but the buttonhole remains.

———

Someone told me about a club where each member had to sign in on every visit. This was because the club had some special liquor licence which made this necessary. But the habit continued long after it was no longer required by the licensing laws.

Tradition is a specific reason for keeping things the way they have always been. In certain cases the value of a tradition may need to be challenged. Tradition is a useful value but does not override all other values. Where tradition is not the reason for keeping things the way they have always been, the reason is often 'simple neglect'.

———

We tend to restrict our thinking to 'problem solving'. It may be that we want to do something and the 'problem' is how to do it, or how to overcome some obstacle. It may be that the problem is a deviation from the normal and we seek to solve the problem.

If something is not a problem it does not get any thinking time. It is as simple as that. Many ways of doing things survive for years because they are adequate. There is nothing wrong; there is not a problem. So why should we think about them? Why should we give such matters any attention at all? It is only when there is a motivated search for simplicity that we start to look at things which are not problems and start to ask: 'Is that really the simplest way to do things?'

That some way of doing things has survived over time does not mean that it is the best way or the simplest way. It may only mean that no one has yet tried to find a better way.

We consider that if something has survived over time it must be the best way, otherwise it would not have survived. We also believe that the process of evolution will have moulded it into the best way. Neither of these assumptions is correct. Most things survive because they are adequate; because they are not problems; and because no one has set out to challenge them. They may be far from the simplest way of doing things.

——————

It may also be that things were done in a certain way because at the time the technology was not available to do them any differently. Today, computers and telecommunications may allow us to do things in a totally different way. For example, the Internet allows education at home in a way that was never possible before. This need not mean that children sit at home watching the Internet instead of going to school, but it could mean that for one day a week children work at home on their Internet assignments while the school helps those youngsters who need extra help.

——————

Historical review means examining each part of a process, operation or item to see how it actually came about in the first place. Sometimes we may know; sometimes there may be documentation; and sometimes we may just have to speculate.

Have we always done it this way?

How did it come to be done this way, in the first place?

Do we really need to continue to do it this way?

——————

Sometimes we adjust
so well to the current
way of doing things
that any change seems
unthinkable.

Airlines started well before the computer age. The whole business of ticketing, reservation and check-in procedures are really pre-computer in concept and execution. The whole procedure could be greatly simplified today – as is happening with electronic tickets. The trouble is that because of the frequent breakdowns of existing computer systems, no one is very keen to transfer all activities to computers. An optional system could be designed allowing either of the channels to be used.

The limitation of baggage weight on airlines was put in place when the older propeller driven aircraft did have a restricted load capacity. This is no longer the case with jet planes. The load limitation stays in place, partly to prevent an abuse of unlimited luggage and partly because there is revenue to be had from overweight luggage.

Our systems of democracy and law are very antiquated. It is absurd to imagine that we could not design simpler, fairer and more effective systems. We dare not try because such subjects are taboo and must never be reconsidered.

We fear that any change would only be in the direction of some vested interests. We also fear unforeseeable consequences. So on balance we prefer the 'devil we know' to the new one we do not know. The perceived risk of change locks us into systems that become increasingly unable to cope with the demands put on them – as in the lawcourts.

As a ship's hull attracts barnacles, so all processes attract complications and additions which add little value.

In essence, historical review is a straightforward procedure. We look to see if something is being done simply because it was done yesterday and in the past. If we come to the conclusion that it is being done because no one has thought to re-examine it, then we might want to change or drop it. If we come to the conclusion that it is being done for the sake of tradition, then we can assess whether in this case tradition is a sufficient reason for keeping things complex.

Shedding, slimming, cutting and trimming

'Can we cut this?'
'Can we drop this?'
'Let's just stop doing this.'

Historical review is obviously just a special case of the more general 'shedding' procedure. In historical review we throw something out because the reason for doing it was historical and no longer exists today. In the more general procedure, we do exactly the same thing but we throw something out because there is no need for it.

For perhaps fifty years they used to charge a toll on each side of a particular bridge. Then one day they decided that since most cars going across were eventually going to return, it was enough to charge only at one end – which is what happens today.

'Why are we doing this?'
'Do we really need to do this?'

Every aspect is reviewed and 'asked' to justify its continued existence. This is what is sometimes called 'zero-based' assessment. Nothing is taken for granted or assumed to be essential unless it is actually found to be so.

In this approach we seek to 'shed' something completely, not to find an alternative way of doing it. Minor adjustments may need to be made.

It takes a lot of determination to look at things which seem so obviously to be essential and to 'ask' them to justify their continuation.

————————

The purest form of the 'shedding' approach simply involves throwing things out and putting nothing in their place. Someone comes in wearing a dress covered in bows. You tear off the bows and leave a more elegant dress behind.

This pure form is quite rare. Usually there will be a need for some adjustment after you have thrown out some aspect of the operation. If you throw out examinations in schools you may want to increase the process of continuous assessment.

If you are simply throwing something out in order to find a different way of doing the same thing, that is not part of the 'shedding' process but a matter of finding alternative methods.

In making official speeches at conferences it is normal to greet all the dignitaries present as a matter of courtesy. I tend to ignore this, not out of rudeness, but because no one has bothered to list them for me and as a guest speaker it is not expected of me.

I have about five university degrees but I do not include any of them on my business card. It is simpler that way and my use of a business card is rather different from other people's use. I am usually giving the card to people who already know me.

Sometimes there are hidden reasons behind things which are not easily seen. When car-park machines ask you to take your ticket there is no functional reason behind this except that if you did not take your ticket the tickets would create litter someone else would have to clear up.

You challenge the idea
that it needs doing at all
or that this is the only
way of doing it.

Challenge is never, never,
never an attack.

The challenge process

The challenge process is part of lateral thinking. It is a very simple process but like all simple processes, some people find it difficult to use.

The challenge process is a key part of the 'shedding' approach.

With 'challenge' you look at something and you say to yourself: 'That may be the best way of doing things, that may even be the only way of doing things – but I want to challenge it.'

Challenge is always directed at what exists now, both in the external world and also in our current thinking.

Challenge is never an attack. Challenge never points out deficiencies, inadequacies or problems.

There are three types of 'why' that underline the challenge process:

'Why C' stands for 'cut'. Do we need to do this at all? Can we just drop it?

'Why B' stands for 'because'. What are the reasons for doing things this way? Do we still have to follow those reasons?

'Why A.' A challenge to 'uniqueness'. Are there 'alternative' ways of doing it?

In 1971 I was doing some work with a major oil company. I said: 'Why do you drill oil wells straight down? Why don't you have wells which bend horizontally at a certain depth?'

There was no problem with existing oil wells, but challenge is not directed only at problems. Anything at all can be challenged. You

A challenge to the way oil wells are drilled resulted in a yield between three and six times what it had been before.

If unnecessary things add to clarity or simplicity they should be retained.

could challenge the reason why spectacle lenses are the same size for each eye.

Today, almost all oil wells are drilled exactly as I suggested – because you get between three and six times as much oil from such wells. I am certainly not claiming that this change was due to my suggestion, which was probably instantly forgotten. I am using it as an example of a challenge which turned out to be very valuable.

For the 'shedding' process the Why C and Why B are the most relevant aspects of challenge because we are not immediately concerned with substituting an alternative. We just want to get rid of what is no longer necessary and what clutters things up.

Sometimes things are 'unnecessary' or 'redundant'. Does the challenge process mean that we have to throw out such things? Not at all.

If the things that are redundant add to the complexity of the situation, they may be thrown out. If the redundancy clarifies or simplifies the matter, then it should be retained even if it is unnecessary. There is never any harm in putting up too many direction signposts.

Why do books have covers, which may (or may not) add to the cost of production? The cover may be there to hold attracting pictures or to make the book easier to hold. Usually the cover is there for protection. If the reason was mainly 'protection', we could shed the cover and simply print four first pages and four last pages. When the top page got dirty you would simply tear it off and have a clean page underneath.

The people who are actually using the process may well have developed short cuts and simplifications over time.

The lazier a person is, the more likely is that person to seek simpler ways to do things.

Listening

The process of 'listening' is part of the two previous approaches but also has value in its own right.

You simply listen to people working at the 'sharp end'. You listen to the people who are using the actual process.

You may find that some things are simply ignored. Sometimes short cuts have developed. At other times people go through certain motions only because they are expected to.

A powerful approach to simplifying anything is to listen to the people who are carrying through the operation.

This approach is not infallible. Sometimes the operators have got so used to carrying through the routine that they have been taught that they have never stopped to challenge that routine. Using a prescribed routine is simpler than figuring everything out from scratch.

If you can identify 'lazy' people, it might be best to listen to such people. They are the ones who are motivated to make life easier for themselves. They are the ones who are motivated to make things simpler.

Again there are dangers. People who have developed short cuts might well be endangering safety (quite often) and quality. Nevertheless it is worth listening to them.

You do not only have to listen passively. You can also ask questions. You can also ask people to think about what they are doing with a view to making it more simple. You can set up small task forces to seek to simplify any operation.

Simplification can arise
from knowing the job
intimately; from a
'standback' perspective;
or even from an innocent
look at the job.

You do not need to provide all the brainpower yourself. Other people also have brains and can be encouraged to use them. Which they will do if they know that you are 'listening'.

On-the-job simplification suggestions can be very helpful. At the same time it can also be helpful to step back and to look at the job from an overall perspective. Both are valuable. Sometimes it can even be valuable to ask a worker to look at someone else's job. The fresh and innocent view might also lead to simplifications.

In all cases it needs to be made clear that 'simplicity' is the value that is being sought. People are being asked to 'simp'.

Sometimes you need to listen with your eyes rather than your ears. You stand and watch (or video) someone doing a task and you observe what short cuts and simplifications are actually being made. A person may not be able to express these verbally because that person may have forgotten what the more complicated process was meant to be.

Suggestion schemes are powerful if they are run well. If such schemes are just left in the background, as part of the furniture, they will not work. It is not enough to promise rewards to 'great ideas' that eventually save money. Most people do not believe they will ever have such 'great ideas', so they do not bother.

In a suggestion scheme you need to reward effort and then you will get results. It does not work the other way around.

The important thing is to reward effort, not results. If you reward effort, you will get results. If you only reward results, you will not get effort.

So it is important to acknowledge all suggestions – even the most useless. This gets energy into the system.

It is also useful to vary the focus from month to month. It is difficult to be creative about everything all the time. So you set specific focuses which narrow the field of thinking.

From time to time, suggestion schemes can be focused directly on 'simplicity' as the desired value.

A mountain top can be reached by various routes. Some are easier than others. You do not use all of them at the same time. You select and try.

Chapter 8

Three More Ways to Work towards Simplicity:

– Combining

– Extracting Concepts

– Bulk and Exceptions

Functions are usually separate because they have been designed separately and no one has thought of them as a whole.

Combining different functions and operations

If you had to make a separate visit to the supermarket for each item you needed that would be very tedious and complicated. We combine the journeys into one – and may even use a shopping list. Possibly, combination could go even further and several neighbours could combine their shopping needs so that one person, in turn, does the bulk shopping. The role of 'professional shopper' is emerging to do shopping for several people.

The Australian Centrelink concept of combining different welfare agencies under one heading is an example of simplification through combining.

In the future all different credit and debit cards might be combined in one card with an in-built electronic chip so that you only need to carry one card. You would then route it as you wished.

A combined ticket and boarding card (to be scanned electronically) would make air travel somewhat simpler.

In hot countries with a high humidity ordinary air conditioners could produce a huge amount of top-quality water – if they were asked to. So the cooling and water functions would be combined.

A busker entertaining a queue may play three or four musical instruments at one time. The arrangements are highly ingenious. This may be carrying combination beyond simplicity and towards complication.

Combination may simply be an 'add-on' process. You put some things in a shopping basket and then you put some more things into the same basket. The items do not interact. You are simply

Combination may mean
adding things together
like potatoes on a plate.
Or it could mean
integrating the functions
as in a good soup.

placing them together. If you could carry out 'postal matters' when you went to the bank – or the other way round – this would simply be adding the functions together. In some countries post offices are indeed used for financial matters.

If whenever you had your teeth checked the dentist routinely checked your weight and blood pressure, that would be an add-on combination.

————

There is another type of combination where the two functions are more closely integrated. Many, many years ago I suggested that supermarkets, instead of giving discounts to loyal, high-purchasing customers, could pay for life-insurance premiums. I believe this is now being done – quite independently of my suggestion.

There are now all sorts of 'affinity' cards. When you use these debit cards for shopping a small part of the money spent goes to a specified charity.

Being able to book hotels and car rentals at the same time as an airline ticket would make life simpler. This could be an 'add-on' or there could be a totally new type of 'travel ticket' which served all these functions.

————

I have often suggested that books should be sold in restaurants. On the menu, or on an inserted slip, would be listed a number of useful books (including this one). A diner would simply order a book in addition to ordering the meal. A host could order a book and give it as a present to the guest. It would all be paid for on the same bill.

Combination could make it simpler to do what you already have to do or it could make it simpler to do more things. The first use is more relevant here.

While the 'browsing' aspect of book buying is increasingly well looked after, the specific purchase is still much too complicated. If you want to go to a bookshop and just look around to see what might interest you, that is well organized. But if you want to go to a bookshop to buy a specific book, that is much too complicated. You have to search and locate the section and the book, and may then find that it is out of stock. You should be able to phone in and have the book ready to be picked up at a special pick-up desk, or have it delivered to you. The simplicity of book ordering and delivery via the Internet is responsible for the great success of Amazon.com.

Driving and listening to audio tapes is a good example of combined functions. Hands-free cellular communication is another example. In both cases, however, there is the risk of lessened attention to driving.

In all cases of 'combining' there is always the underlying question: 'Does this really make things simpler, does it make things more complex, or does it simply allow you to do more?'

The pure example is where two different functions both have to be carried out. If these two operations can be combined, then only one operation has to be carried out. If you could shave, clean your teeth and brush your hair all in one operation, life would be a little bit simpler. If you could study and have fun and enjoy your friends all at the same time, education would be a lot simpler.

Some people are impatient with concepts and regard them as academic and abstract. Such people prefer concrete hands-on action. They do not realize that the purpose of concepts is to breed concrete alternatives for action.

Extracting concepts

This may well be the most important process of all when you are trying to simp. Unfortunately, many people are extremely uncomfortable with 'concepts'. Such people do not like vague concepts. They want 'hands-on', concrete reality. Concepts are a hugely important part of thinking and of creative thinking in particular.

I doubt very much whether there is any truth in the following story but it does illustrate the point.

Ballpoint pens cannot write upside down for any length of time. Ballpoint pens depend on gravity to feed the ink and writing tip, so ballpoints do not function very well on space missions where there may be no gravity. The task was therefore to design a ballpoint pen that would work well in space. At some cost this pen was designed. It is a brilliant little pen that is now generally for sale. Nitrogen under pressure supplies the ink and gravity is not needed.

It is said (and it is probably untrue) that the Russian space pro-gramme reached the same point. But instead of setting out to design a gravity-free ballpoint, they used a concept. They said to themselves: 'We want something that writes upside down.'

So they used a pencil.

———————

You are driving along a road to the beach. When you get there you find that the beach is noisy, crowded, dirty, etc. You believe that other parts of the long beach will be more attractive. There is no road running along the beach. So what do you do? You drive back to the nearest roundabout (rotary) and from this take another road to a different part of the beach.

Most of the excellent
qualities of the brain
arise directly from
poor engineering.

You cannot think of
alternatives without there
being a background
concept in your mind.

Concepts are the junctions in the mind. Concepts are the round-abouts in the mind. Once you get back to the roundabout you can take a different route.

The ability to form concepts, like almost all the excellent behaviour of the human brain, arises from poor engineering. An engineer could never have designed the human brain. An engineer would have thrown out all those features which specifically give the human brain its immense ability.

Concepts arise from the inability of the brain to form precise images. Who would want a camera that only took very blurred photographs? These blurred images form the concepts. At the same time the brain has dynamic processing – it uses 'water logic', not traditional 'rock logic'. Traditional logic is the logic of identity: 'What is this?' Water logic is the logic of flow: 'Where does this lead to?' (*See* my book *Water Logic*.) This allows the brain to have all the benefits of blurred and fuzzy processing and at the same time great precision.

Whenever we set out to look for alternatives there is always a 'background' concept in our minds. You cannot begin to look for alternatives without a background concept. Usually, we are not clearly aware of what that concept might be.

In my seminars I sometimes ask people for different ways of dividing a square into four equal pieces. One of the simplest ways is to divide the square into four slices. Almost everyone uses this approach – and then goes on to look for further approaches such as diagonals, quarters and so on.

The 'four-slice' approach is seen as just one way of dividing the

What is the operating concept here? How else can we put that concept into action?

square into four equal pieces. Very few people pause to consider this four-slice approach. What concept do we have here?

The concept is actually very simple and very powerful. If you divide the square into half, then you can divide each half into half any way you like. There are now a huge number of ways of dividing each half into half.

Indeed, there is another concept. Any line which passes through the centre of each half and is repeated above and below that centre will divide the half into half again.

――――――

'If that is what we are trying to do, then we could probably do it in a much simpler way.'

The value of 'extracting' the operating concept is that we might be able to find a simpler way of carrying out that concept.

What is the operating concept behind parking meters in cities? Is it just a way of raising revenue? This is probably not the operating concept, because the cost of maintaining and monitoring the meters absorbs all the revenue produced. The concept is possibly that of 'allowing as many people as possible to make use of limited parking space'. In other words, you do not want early morning commuters to take a space and sit in it all day long to the extent that shoppers and others have no place to park.

If we are happy that this is indeed the operating concept, then we look around for a simpler way to deliver that concept.

One very simple way of carrying out this defined operating concept is to say: 'You can park in any designated space you like for as long as you like – provided you leave the car headlights full on!'

Once you have extracted the concept you can clarify it, improve it, change it and redesign it.

If the operating concept remains hidden you remain dominated by it.

No one is going to want to leave their car with headlights on for any length of time because they would run the batteries down. So people will limit their parking as much as they can. There is no need to install meters and monitoring is much simpler.

Of course, there would be a lot of objections to this suggestion. Dazzled by headlights; difficulty in removing cars with flat batteries; waste of energy; cheating by having spare batteries in the boot of the car – these are just some of the objections. The basic concept of 'self limiting' can, however, be carried out in other simpler and more practical ways.

Once you have 'extracted' the concept you can clarify it, change it, improve it or even redesign it. Then you seek alternative ways of putting the concept into practical action. Some of the processes of lateral thinking (like the 'concept fan') are based directly on this process. You work backwards from the objective using concepts which get more and more specific until you end up with a usable idea. (*See* my *Serious Creativity*.)

Concepts have to be 'general', 'vague' and 'blurry'. That is their function. In that way you can move out of a concept in many possible directions. If a concept is detailed and concrete you cannot move anywhere.

People, especially Americans, tend to be impatient with concepts, precisely because they are abstract, general, vague and blurry. This is what makes concepts such powerful 'breeders' of practical ideas. Those who are impatient with concepts do not seem to realize the difference between a concept and an idea. There is no intention of using the concept in a practical action sense. The purpose of the concept is only to 'breed' ideas. The ideas themselves do have to be concrete and usable. You cannot stay at the concept level all

It is essential to work with the middle level of concepts. Concepts that are too broad lead nowhere. Concepts that are too narrow lead only down that narrow path.

the time: that would be like saying, 'I am going to solve this problem by using the most appropriate solution.'

———————

Extracting 'operating concept' is by no means easy. If you use too broad a level you get nowhere. At the broadest level the concept behind any business is 'to survive'. At a slightly less broad level you might say 'to make profits'. So, too broad a level of concept covers everything and therefore indicates very little. Too tight a level of concept is down at detail level and you cannot go any-where else. It is the middle level of concept that is the most valuable. Using this middle level is as much art as science. It is useful to be conscious that your concepts may be either too broad or too narrow.

———————

There may be several, parallel operating concepts. In a shop there are at least three parallel concepts: display and selection; stock of items; convenience of purchase. We could separate these out. You could do your selection by catalogue, by video or by Internet. You could order by phone and then go to pay and pick up at a 'collection point'. Or, the whole operation could be by mail order. In the USA the mail-order business has a bigger turnover than the automobile industry. Originally the mail-order business thrived because people in rural areas could not easily get to stores or because the local stores could not stock a wide enough range of items because of low local demand. Today, the convenience aspect coupled with excellent delivery systems is the attraction. Where both partners work there is less time for shopping and there may be preferred ways of spending leisure time.

With television shopping the biggest sale item is jewellery. This can become a self-fulfilling prophecy. If jewellery sells well, then more

You cannot analyse your way to concepts. You have to create them as possibilities in your mind – then you will see them around you.

time is devoted to selling jewellery, so it does become the biggest selling item, etc. What concept might be involved here?

Jewellery stores, and their staff, are intimidating. You do not want to be persuaded to buy at a higher price than you intended. You do not want to feel embarrassed by spending too little. The choices in a jewellery shop are too great. On television you are shown one thing at a time – and usually it seems a good bargain. It may also look better on television than in real life, especially as regards size.

Perhaps the most powerful concept is that 'you are giving yourself a present'. You order it and then, one day, it arrives – just as if someone had sent you a present. It is also a very convenient way of giving presents to other people. Through experience the price range of 'present giving' has also been carefully assessed, which is not the case in a jewellery store.

––––––––

The operating concepts behind 'fast food' might be: location and ease of access; brand identification; high standards; predictable food; predictable prices; quick service, etc. These might be summarized as 'convenience' and 'predictability' (food, standard, price, service, etc.).

Working from such concepts we might devise an alternative business: a fast-food chain with no outlets at all. The food would be branded and predictable in standard, type and price. Any eating establishment could have a notice in the window saying: 'We sell Joe's Food at Joe's price.' Quality would need to be sustained through inspections, complaint attention, etc.

Systems that seek to cover
all exceptions make it
immensely complicated
for the bulk of people
who are not exceptions.

Deal with the bulk and make provisions for the exceptions

When you are standing in line to go through passport control it always seems that the person in front of you has some immensely complicated problem that is taking ages to sort out. The same thing used to happen in banks and supermarkets.

The single-point queue system is an excellent way of overcoming the problem because you are no longer stuck in one particular line. In supermarkets special check-outs for those with a few items only also help with the problem.

Many systems, particularly laws, are immensely complicated because they have to deal with all sorts of exceptions and imagined types of abuse. If we could just deal with the 'bulk' of situations, the central part of the 'bell curve', then everything could be much simpler.

Clothing stores can no longer afford to carry a wide range of possible sizes. They just carry the 'bulk' sizes. If you are exceptional, then you go to a special store that carries 'outsize' clothes. If you are exceptionally small, you could always try to wear the clothes of youngsters.

———

The great Socrates once asked his pupil: 'What do you mean by "justice"?' The pupil replied: 'Justice is giving back to someone what belongs to that person.'

'Wait a bit,' said Socrates. 'Suppose you borrow a knife from your friend and later that friend becomes mad and violent. Should you give your friend the knife back?'

While operations can be designed for the bulk of users, controls and instructions have to be designed for the most basic of users.

This was a favourite trick of Socrates (and philosophers ever since). He would seek out some very exceptional case in order to show that a definition was not 'absolute'. This was because he insisted on the logic that is based on 'always' and 'never' and 'all' and 'none'.

While this is a very useful system, it also leads to great complexity as we struggle to include all exceptions. A logic based on 'by and large', 'generally' and 'usually' is far more practical, though possibly more difficult in legal matters.

———

Things can often be simplified by designing the system to deal with the 'bulk' of situations and people. Then there are special provisions for dealing with all those situations and people who fall outside this 'average' or bulk use.

There are times when you cannot do this. You cannot design the controls of a car for the 'average' driver and then suggest that 'below average' drivers should buy special cars. You need to design the controls to be used by everyone. That has the effect of making them simpler for everyone – which is no bad thing.

Education sets out to deal with the bulk of students and then makes provision at either end of the curve: the gifted and the remedial. This is practical but has some dangers. Those labelled as 'remedial' lose confidence and have low expectations, which actually reduces their performance. At the other end, if the gifted only socialize with the gifted they lose out on social skills.

———

I have suggested that someone should set up a 'Flexi-bank'. This would be a bank that specialized in dealing with exceptional cases

It is never a matter of designing for the bulk of users and ignoring the exceptions. It is a matter of designing two specific channels: one for the bulk of users and one for the exceptions. Both need to be well designed.

which did not fit into the categorization habits of normal retail banking. Something of the sort did happen when some banks found it highly profitable to lend to people no one else would lend to.

Restaurant menus could be greatly simplified if the range of dishes was reduced to the dishes most ordered. Supplies, storage, cooking, staff would all be simplified. That is, of course, one of the key operating concepts of the fast-food business.

Bookshops and toyshops used to stock a wide range of exotic items – not any more. Today, they focus on the bulk items that move fast. This may be disappointing for a few customers but it does simplify things for the shop.

This particular approach to simplification should not be a matter of ignoring or throwing out the exceptional in order to deal only with the bulk. It is more a matter of designing two channels, both of which are designed to deal with what passes through them. The 'bulk' channel deals with the majority of cases and can be much simplified because that is all it is going to be doing. The 'exceptional' channel is specifically intended to deal with the exceptional cases. It is also designed for that purpose (higher level of training of staff, etc.).

A carpenter can use all the tools of carpentry but at any one moment uses the tool that seems appropriate for the situation.

Chapter 9

More Approaches:

– **Restructuring**

– **Start Afresh**

– **Modules and Smaller Units**

If you are too good at adjusting to the current system you may never realize that the system needs changing.

Innocence is something which no amount of experience can deliver.

Restructuring

Across the big global accountancy firms about 41 per cent of income comes from consultancy. Much of the income of management consultants, quite rightly, comes from advising clients on how to restructure. Sometimes this is termed 're-engineering'.

It is very difficult to restructure from within an organization for a number of good reasons.

1. People within an organization have got so used to the existing structure that they cannot see anything odd or inefficient about it. They are so good at adapting to the existing structure that there is little motivation to change it.

2. You need an outside eye to look 'innocently' at the structure and to wonder why things are done in such a bizarre way.

3. By definition, consultants have experience across many more organizations than any person within an organization is likely to have. So consultants know the pitfalls, dangers, sensitive points, etc.

4. Within an organization there are problems with territories, politics, personalities, etc. An outside agent is not immediately subjected to these.

5. Many people within an organization may want change and may even know what they want to do. But they do not have the political muscle to make it happen. A management consultant is often of value in reflecting back, with far more credibility, what some people already know. If the fee is high enough the consultancy is likely to be believed.

Fashionable models may be well worth adopting provided the reason for adopting them is that they fit. Fashion serves to bring such models to our attention.

6. Any suggested change within an organization is likely to be viewed with suspicion and regarded as arising from the special interest of a person or group of people.

7. Change is trouble, hassle, disruption and new things to learn. No change is a preferred option. If you have learned to play the existing game why should you want the game changed?

—————

Restructuring can simply involve a fashionable model. There is a fashion for 'flattening' organizations. This means removing some of the many layers of middle management. There may be a fashion for decentralization. There may be a fashion for out-sourcing many of the functions now carried on internally: data processing, production, etc. There may be a fashion for breaking up a large organization into smaller units so the stock market can truly appreciate the value of each unit. AT&T in the USA did just this. So did Fletcher Challenge in New Zealand.

Because something is a 'fashion' does not mean that it is bad, unsuitable or unnecessary. Many good things do come about through fashion. Fashion does not create their value but fashion allows the impetus for good things to be taken up and used.

When fashion is the driving force it is well worth looking at the fashionable 'model' and trying it for fit. Fashion is a good reason for looking at something but not a good enough reason for using something. If it makes sense, adopt the model. If it does not make sense, then ignore the fashion.

—————

Almost any proposed model for change can stimulate thinking about things which need to be thought about. This may be more important than the proposed model.

At a less compulsive level than fashion is the 'model' set by one or more specific organizations. These organizations have been successful by doing it this way – maybe we should do it the same way?

If there is the real need for change, which there usually is, then almost any of these approaches will provide benefits, because it means that things are being looked at and are being thought about. The sheer momentum of continuity has been broken. There may even be a fresh energy to make the new model work. There can also be new people in new positions who are eager to use their energies productively.

It may just be that 'change for the sake of change' might show some unexpected benefits.

Of course, there are models which fit well and where the change is fully explored and fully justified. Otherwise management consultants would not be earning their fee, would they?

Keep simplicity in mind

It would be very rare indeed for the restructuring mentioned above to be carried out for the sake of simplifying the structure. Simplicity has not yet reached that level of appreciation as a value. The usual motivations are: cost saving; efficiency; easier communication and productivity. It is also possible that a newly appointed chief executive wants to make his or her mark.

In this whole process 'simplicity' is usually somewhere in the back of people's minds as one of the benefits. It may be useful to bring this forward and to make it overt as one of the acknowledged aims of restructuring. It is true that simplicity can feed into cost cutting, downsizing, ease of communication, flexibility, etc., etc.,

Fundamental restruc-
turing gets very close to
starting afresh. Forget
what we now have, what
are the values we want to
deliver? How are we
going to deliver them?

but it is still worth giving simplicity a value of its own. In other words, amongst the many 'gods' that management worships there should be one called 'simplicity'.

Start afresh

There is a great deal of overlap between restructuring and starting afresh. At one end of the spectrum there is the total new design and at the other end is the attempt to restructure an existing process. The thinking moves backwards and forwards along the spectrum.

'What would we be doing if we were starting afresh and did not have to work with existing systems?'

One day the Japanese food processors got together to simplify the way they were distributing food to the huge number of tiny retail outlets in Japan. (Until recently supermarkets were forbidden by law, in order to preserve the small shops.) A processor might be sending a tiny load in a van to a particular store; another processor might be sending another tiny load in a van to the same store. So they decided to set up a joint distribution system. This one system would now distribute all the goods, and only one van would be visiting the small store – with goods from all the different processors. They ended up saving 80 per cent of their distribution costs.

That is how they would have designed the system if they had been starting afresh.

The design process
consists of knowing where
you want to go, finding
ways of getting there and
considering the various
factors involved.

The design process

It is not my intention here to go through the whole design process but just to outline some of the aspects.

There are four aspects:
1. thrust
2. alternatives
3. considerations
4. modification.

That is only one way of looking at design. There are many other ways.

Thrust . . .

'Thrust' means moving with energy in a defined direction. So under thrust comes a clear sense of what we are trying to do, what we are trying to achieve.

'What are we really trying to do here?'

We need to spell out in words what we are seeking to achieve. If there are multiple thrusts, then we spell them all out. It may not be possible to follow different thrusts at the same time. So we may need to select the dominant thrust and deal with the others later on.

What effect are we seeking to have?

An 'effect' that is positive is called a 'value'.

In the 'tree metaphor' the thrust is the trunk of the tree. Even though the thrust is an abstract intention or a general mechanism it still forms the trunk of the tree.

You can never improve
the quality of your final
choice by limiting the
range of alternatives.
Know how to generate
alternatives and know how
to choose between them.

The scan of considerations
should be as broad as
possible but with a clear
sense of priorities and
relative importance.

Alternatives . . .

Once we know what we want to do and where we want to go, we look around for alternative ways of getting there. These might be standard approaches, which are well known and much used. There might be a linking together of standard approaches. There might be a need to design a special approach. There might even be a need to be creative about designing a new approach.

There is a temptation to settle for the first approach that seems to work. There is a need to resist this temptation and to think further.

'How are we going to carry out this intention (thrust)?'

'What are the alternative ways of doing it?'

The clearer the definition of the thrust, the more chance there is of finding a way of achieving the intention.

The alternatives provide the 'possible' branches of the tree. The real branches will be the method finally chosen for delivering the values intended.

Considerations . . .

One of the DATT tools (Direct Attention Thinking Tools) is called the CAF (Consider All Factors). This is also part of the CoRT thinking lessons for schools.

So at this point we do a wide scan of all the relevant factors: cost, feasibility, legality, acceptance, implementation, etc., etc. Considerations not only include constraints and resources, but may also include intentions. For example, we have the intention of making something 'simple'. That is a key consideration.

Unless simplicity is defined as a priority it will not be there.

If necessary, priorities may be allocated to the considerations so that the key ones can be considered first.

The considerations are now applied to the alternatives in order to see which alternative is best suited to the considerations. This is where priorities may become important. There may be conflicts. There may be a conflict between cost, practicality and value. There may be a conflict between simplicity and practicality.

Such conflicts are either solved by a further design process which seeks to resolve the conflict – or by a straightforward 'trade-off' choice between the different considerations (positive and negative values). It is here that there needs to be an emphasis on simplicity. A wonderful delivery process that is not simple enough may be unacceptable.

Modification . . .

Even when we have decided on the mechanism there may still be a need to modify this mechanism to take into account the various considerations.

The chosen method of delivering the value represent the 'branches' in the tree metaphor. The branches may have to be 'trained' or modified. For example, a particular design solution may not work in a country because of the different life-style habits. So there is a need for a modification.

Occasionally, so much modification is needed that you might as well go back to the alternative stage. Excessive modification usually destroys any simplicity.

There is no point in ending up with a very simple way of delivering nothing. The key values have also to be kept in mind.

When the whole purpose of the 'start afresh' exercise is to simplify something, then the emphasis needs to be on simplicity at every moment.

'Is there a simpler way to do this?'

'Is this really necessary?'

'Does this add to simplicity or increase complexity?'

At the end we do not want a very simple way of delivering nothing. So the values we are trying to deliver cannot be ignored in favour of simplicity. Simplicity is an important consideration and an important operational value – but it is not the only one.

It is important to use 'simplicity' throughout the design process and not just as part of the judgement screen at the end of the process. It is not enough just to keep knocking back designs because they are not simple enough. Unless simplicity is a consideration throughout the design process, you are not going to get simplicity.

Modules and smaller units

Armies are divided into divisions. Divisions contain regiments, regiments are divided into battalions and battalions into platoons. Where an overall organization is going to be much too complex it is standard procedure to divide the organization up into smaller units. The same thing holds in government with local councils, mayors, etc. So one approach to simplification is to divide the overall structure into sub-units.

In the investment world there are times when analysts praise the collecting of smaller units into one big conglomerate. Analysts talk up the stock value of this aggregation. Some time later the same

The organization of the
human body depends on
tiny sub-units called cells.
Each cell has its own
organization but also fits
into the total organization
both in terms of main-
tenance and also moment-
to-moment action.

Where there is no natural
division into smaller units it
may be difficult to impose
this on an existing
structure.

analysts talk up the value of breaking down the conglomerate into smaller units which may be sold off separately. The same thing happens over and again. This is not surprising. Analysts and investors make their money in a fluctuating market. If everything is stable it is difficult to be a smart investor. And at each part of the cycle the arguments put forward by the analysts are logical and perfectly correct. There are advantages to aggregating smaller units. There are advantages in breaking down big units into smaller units.

In the human body each individual cell is an organization unit. These units form part of bigger units (glands, muscles, bone). Each cell is affected by chemical messengers sent out by headquarters. Each part may also be affected by electrical signals coming down the nerves. The body is a marvellous model of a centralized and decentralized system.

The organization of a small unit can be relatively simple. The relationship of a smaller unit to the whole can also be relatively simple. In this way a complex organization is much simplified.

Local telephone exchanges are an obvious example of decentralization. A signal is routed through regional and then local exchanges and finally to the receiver.

In big cities there is a constant effort to build 'smaller communities'. In the small community of a village, people look after each other. In a big city the organization unit is much too large. There is a real need for smaller units. But it is far from easy to get them because there is no natural basis for the smaller unit and artificial attempts are ignored by most people. Perhaps pavements (sidewalks) should be painted different colours in different areas to give some sense of difference.

Decentralization may lead to simplicity in operation but increased complexity in administration.

It may not be easy to break down a large organization unit into smaller sub-units. The roles and lines of communication all have to be altered. The responsibilities will be changed. Power will be changed. Support is only likely to come from those who may move up to head the smaller units. Senior management is unlikely to want to delegate power.

If you take all aspects of organization into consideration it may actually be that decentralization leads to more complexity – in a sense. Australia is said to be the most over-governed country in the world. There are possibly more politicians per head of the population in Australia than anywhere else in the world. There is a central federal government in Canberra – with two chambers. Then each state has its own full arrangement of parliamentary power with its own premier. Being a vast country made up of hitherto more or less independent states, something of the sort is necessary. Yet if you count up the number of politicians and administrative layers you might find the decentralized system to be more complex in itself than a centralized one, although it may still be simpler in operation.

Modules

Modules are sub-units which have their own 'life' and organization, but come together to give an overall function. There are many advantages to modules:

1. Ease of manufacture and assembly of sub-units, including out-sourcing.

2. Assembly of different modules in different combinations to give different products.

3. Possibility of adding on modules to give additional functions (as in computers).

Modules can offer simplicity in many directions, from production to repair.

Modules need to be specifically designed. Modules are more than just parts of the whole.

4. Ease of diagnosis if things go wrong. Each module can be tested in its own right. Sometimes modules can be designed to be self-testing.

5. Ease of repair. A faulty module is simply replaced.

There are also disadvantages, such as a lot of redundancy; the inability to make full use of specialized central functions; more assembly work being required in total; possibly less 'fine' flexibility, etc.

———————

With regard to simping structures, modularization may be a good way to go. A car put together from modules may be less pleasing aesthetically but easier to produce, easier to repair and easier to customize. Consumers would, however, be hesitant to buy such a car because aesthetics and 'individuality' play such a large part in car purchase.

Modules do need to be specifically designed. It is not just a matter of carving up something into chunks and calling these modules. Each module has to be designed to carry out its own part of the organization.

Sub-assemblies are not true modules. They are parts of the whole and when put together no longer function as separate units. Sub-assemblies are 'modules' only during the stage of manufacture (and repair). Instead of everyone working on the car itself, different teams work simultaneously on sub-assemblies, which are then brought together. This can be a great simplification of the production process.

It is essential to be very clear where, why and for whose benefit simplicity is being sought.

As always with simplicity it is essential to be clear where and why simplicity is being sought.

Is it simplicity of production?

Is it simplicity of use?

Is it simplicity of maintenance?

Is it simplicity of operation?

Is it simplicity of repair?

And there are others. The operators of a system are not always the same as the users. The pilot of a plane is not the same as the passengers. The storekeeper is not the same as the consumers. In the case of a motor car the operator and user may indeed be the same.

It may be possible to cover many of the directions of simplicity with one design. But it is still very important to keep the different directions clear in your mind. Is the tax system going to be simplified for the benefit of the taxpayers or for the benefit of the revenue service?

———

Where local flexibility of response is important, then decentralization greatly simplifies the process. Otherwise there would have to be a feedback to central headquarters and the suggested response would probably be inappropriate. The ability of a local unit to respond locally is simpler and more effective. If overall flexibility of response is required, then the opposite holds true. It is much easier to change direction centrally than to have to persuade all local units also to change direction. As at so many other points,

There is no one right
answer to be found.
There are possibilities to
be generated. You
then design forward
from these possibilities.

there is no one right answer that suits all situations. It is a matter of being aware of possibilities and then designing an approach that fits a particular need.

With a 'provocation'
there may not be a reason
for saying something until
after it has been said.

Chapter 10

Further Approaches:

– Provocative Amputation

– Wishful Thinking

– Shift Energies

We do not challenge elements to justify their existence, we just 'amputate' elements arbitrarily and then look to see what happens.

Provocative amputation

Although at first sight this may seem similar to the 'shedding' process described earlier, it is in fact very different.

With the shedding process, or historical review, we look to see if something is really necessary. If it is not really necessary we drop it, discard it or throw it out. The basis for this rejection is that the element is superfluous. You do not throw anything out until you are sure it is superfluous.

With the 'amputation' procedure there is no such examination. We look at all things, one at a time, and then see what would happen if we were to throw out (amputate) that element. There is no need for any justification. Even the most obvious things are 'thrown out'.

The purpose of the shedding process is to leave something simpler and cleaner. The purpose of the 'amputation' process is 'provocation'.

What happens if we drop this?

This process of provocative amputation is very similar to the 'escape' process in lateral thinking.

Provocation and movement

We know that in any self-organizing system, like the human brain, there is a mathematical need for 'provocation'. Otherwise we get stuck in 'local equilibrium' states. From this consideration arise the formal methods of provocation in lateral thinking – *see* the book *Serious Creativity* and also the APTT training courses (*see* page i).

In lateral thinking 'movement' is almost the exact opposite of judgement.

The word 'po' was an invention needed in language to signal a provocation.

There are formal and deliberate methods of setting up provocations and also formal ways of using provocations. The process by which we move forward from a provocation to a useful idea is called 'movement'. This is an 'active' mental operation – not just a suspension of judgement. There are various systematic ways of getting movement (extract a principle, focus on the difference, special circumstances, etc.). 'Movement' is a skill that we need to develop. We hardly use this skill at all in normal life, where everything is based on judgement and identification. Perhaps the only time we use 'movement' is in reading poetry, where we seek to move forward from what the poet writes.

The 'escape' process is one of the formal ways of setting up a provocation. We pick out something that we 'take for granted' in the situation and then we drop or 'escape' from this.

We take it for granted that cars have steering wheels.
Escape: (po) cars do not have steering wheels.

We take it for granted that air travellers have tickets.
Escape: (po) air travellers do not have tickets.

The word 'po' is a word I invented about twenty-five years ago to signal a provocation. There is a need for such a word in language if we are to use provocations. Otherwise anything we say is immediately subjected to judgement rather than 'movement'.

———

The provocative amputation process is very similar. We drop or cancel something that we 'take for granted'. We then look to see

Like many of the other approaches, the 'amputation' process forces us to look more closely at what we take for granted.

what adjustments now become necessary. This sort of thinking can lead to a simplification of the process.

If air passengers did not have tickets, this could lead on to some electronic check-in at the departure gate. There would be no need for an electronic ticket. The passenger would simply key in an identifying code and the travel identifying code and the computer would let the passenger through.

If sales people could not use cars, what would this lead to? There could be telephone selling; selling via the Internet; local sales people; and prospective purchasers being invited to travel to a demonstration and sales point.

If restaurants did not have chairs people would spend less time in the restaurant. This would lead on to the concept of not charging for the food but charging by time. This would enable the food to be cheap and the turnover to be high in places where there was a high demand and limited physical space. This is an example of the provocation of lateral thinking.

If supermarkets did not have checkout points, what would follow? There could be automatic price readers on shopping carts and an 'honour system', with spot checks.

If supermarkets did not have shelves, there might be a demonstration room with samples and video screen and ordering would be done by computer. There could also be 'catalogue shopping' by phone from home, quoting the product code.

It does not necessarily follow that this 'amputation' process will lead to simpler ways of doing things. It is possible that the suggested way is even more complex. What matters is that there has to be some new thinking about the process.

The first idea that comes to mind may not be so interesting but the second and third ideas that flow from it can be very interesting.

Quite often the first idea that comes to mind is not so simple but then simpler ideas flow from this first idea.

———————

The suggestion that a school should have 'no teachers' leads to the immediate idea of staying at home and studying via the Internet or through correspondence courses. But the idea that follows could be a school that is fully set up for distance learning but which has 'learning facilitators' rather than teachers. These facilitators help the students use the distance-learning capabilities. That may be a very different skill from teaching. It may also be a skill for which more people can be trained. Does this simplify the process of education or make it more complex?

The idea lowers the demands on the teacher and can make it simpler for students to get the very best instruction. It may, however, make life more complex for the student, who has now to do more than just sit back and listen.

A manufacturer with 'no production facilities' immediately suggests 'out-sourcing'. The next idea would be joint production facilities owned by a number of producers and producing a range of items.

In lateral thinking 'wishful thinking' should be an extreme fantasy. In the simplication process wishful thinking can be more realistic. Why can't we use this ideal approach?

Wishful thinking

This process is also very similar to the 'wishful thinking' way of setting up a provocation in lateral thinking.

Po, wouldn't it be nice if a factory was downstream of itself on a river.

This 'wishful thinking provocation' leads to the idea that the factory's intake should always be downstream of its own output, so that the factory would be the first to suffer from its own pollution.

Wishful thinking means putting forward an 'ideal' or 'perfect' way of doing things.

Two things can then happen. The first is that you look around to see why this perfect solution cannot be implemented. The second thing is that you use the wish as a provocation to open up new ideas.

The phrase 'wouldn't it be nice if . . .' is a convenient way of expressing wishful thinking.

In lateral thinking, the wishful thought should really be a fantasy that you do not expect ever to become possible; the more extreme the idea, the more productive the provocation. The simplification process is a little different. Here the wishful thought can be quite realistic.

'Wouldn't it be nice if people had exact change when paying for parking.'

This could lead to the idea of some card that was charged up magnetically and could be used for parking and many other purposes that needed small change. The reading machine would

Wishful thinking does have to go beyond a known alternative. It is not just a matter of suggesting an alternative approach. The thought must lead reality forward.

simply deduct the amount from the card. From this comes the idea that parking machines might simply (by arrangement) use telephone cards. Of course, they could also use credit cards, etc., but for small amounts the 'charged' up card is much simpler to administer.

Although the 'wishful thinking' should be realistic this does not mean that you have to know a way of doing it before saying it. It really does need to be 'wishful'.

'Wouldn't it be nice if in a restaurant you could have only the amount you wanted to eat?'

From this might come the idea that you order by price and not just by dish. At the moment, in most restaurants, the price of each dish is listed on the menu. A plate of spaghetti might cost $8. Instead you could order $3 worth of spaghetti. You would get an amount proportional to your chosen price. This would make life more complex for the restaurant owner but simpler for the diner.

Shift energies

In many of the examples given the reader will have noticed that there has been a 'shift of energies'. In the restaurant example, matters are made simpler for the diner but, possibly, more complex for the restaurant owner. In the example of air passengers without tickets the energy of 'complication' has been shifted to a computer system that can verify the passenger and the journey.

There are cars that will automatically adjust to suit a particular driver. The seat is adjusted, the angle of steering wheel, etc. There are cars which will test your breath for alcohol and refuse to start if you are over the limit.

There is a shift of the
energy absorbing com-
plication to a computer, a
machine or someone else.

Simplification for you
may be achieved by
increased complication
elsewhere.

Many not very bright people drive a car which is really a very complex system. The early days of motor cars demanded a great deal from the driver. The energy of 'complication' has been taken away from the driver and given to the car.

In the old days the US embassies used to keep records of when visa applications were made. Then they just stamped the documents and gave the storage function back to the applicant.

Once you are clear what you are trying to simp, then it becomes easier to shift energies so that complication moves from one point to another.

———————

There are now agencies which will make restaurant bookings for you. At busy times you might have had to make several phone calls to make a reservation. All that energy is now shifted to the agency who makes all the phone calls. The service is free and presumably gets a commission from the restaurants.

A competent travel agent is a similar shift of energy. Interestingly, the development of the Internet now means that individuals can make direct airline and hotel reservations via the Internet. So the energy has shifted back to individuals, who find it simpler, now, to be in control of the whole process.

———————

Energy does not have to be shifted to computers or machines. You can also shift the energy of complication to other people. You can delegate. The emergence of 'professional shoppers', who will do all the shopping for you, is an example.

What is needed is not more technology design but more 'value concept' design. Technology can deliver almost any value we design – but we are lagging far behind in the design of value.

With increased automation there is less need for people in production and so people shift into service areas. When the cost of personal service becomes 'tax deductible' (as it surely will, in order to reduce unemployment), then the people earning high incomes will be able to distribute that income in exchange for personal services. This is a traditional way of making life simpler – and also benefits everyone.

A Swedish neurosurgeon will paint his own house because the after-tax costs of employing a painter is so very high. This means the surgeon has less leisure time or less surgery time. Also, the painter does not have a job.

Shifting energies by delegation is really a form of 'modularization' or decentralization.

Instead of doing everything yourself you set up a 'unit' to carry out certain functions (support or enterprise).

Increasingly the shift of energy will be to computers. Computer matching and dating may take much of the complication out of courtship.

The technology of computers is today far in advance of the value concepts we ask computers to deliver. What is needed is not more technology design but more 'value design'. That is going to be the key area of advance. As I said at the TED conference in Monterey, California, in 1997, the information age is over – we are now into the concept age (the design of value).

There will need to be redundancy and back-up systems, otherwise

The fact that computers
can handle complexity
does not mean that we
do not need to design for
simplicity.

a breakdown in computer systems would cause chaos – as happens at airports when the computers are not working.

At the same time there is still a need for 'simplification of design'. It is not enough to say that computers can handle all manner of complexity and so simplification is no longer required. Simple systems are more powerful and more robust. The interface with people must also be extremely simple.

It is possible to work with detail or to work with a very broad approach. Both approaches are valid and available to be used.

No one expects one golf club to do the work of all the others.

Chapter 11

The Last Two Approaches:

The Ladder Approach

The Flavour Approach

We should not assume that simplicity always depends on major changes. Slight changes in small things can sometimes make things much simpler.

The ladder approach

The point about a ladder is that you can eventually rise to a great height by making one small step at a time.

This approach is almost the exact opposite of 'start afresh' or any grand restructuring. Instead, there is an attempt to make each small process, or part of a process, somewhat simpler. This is very similar to the Japanese *kaizen* process of gradual quality improvement. There is a continuous and continuing effort to make each action simpler. Quality remains a key 'direction' but simplicity joins it as a key direction for improvement.

It is obvious that where a major restructuring is needed in order to make things simpler, the 'ladder approach' is unlikely to deliver such a major change. But we should not assume that simplicity always depends on 'major changes'. There are times when a succession of small simping steps can make things simpler both for the operator and also for the customer.

For example, adequate signs can make life much simpler, and putting up such signs is not a major restructuring operation.

———

The advantage of the 'ladder approach' is that everyone can get involved. Each person can think about his or her own job and about his or her own 'interface' with other people.

A bird makes its nest as comfortable as it can for itself and its young. Why should a worker not seek to make life as easy as possible for himself or herself. There is no necessary contradiction between making work easier and productivity. In fact, productivity can increase when work is made easier and simpler.

It is a perfectly legitimate
use of creativity to make
things better not just
for investors or for
customers, but for the
workers themselves.
Better may mean simpler.

Everyone talks about productivity and customer service. Making life easier for the workers themselves is equally legitimate. The use of creativity for simplification is one way this can be done.

In many cafés in Italy you queue up to pay for what you are going to have and then you queue up again to get served at the counter. This was also the system in stores in the old Soviet Union. This process clearly makes life easier for the servers because they do not have to deal both with the items and also with money. The customer, however, has to queue twice. The queues may, of course, be much faster than if the server also had to deal with money. A slight simplification would be the ability to buy standard vouchers in advance. These vouchers would cover your usual preferred food and drink. You would go straight to the serving point and just turn in a pre-paid voucher. A variation would be to have a ticket which could be clipped to indicate usage of certain amounts of money. These are small changes.

Once people start thinking about what they are doing, then it soon becomes clear that some operations are more complex than they need to be.

A simple classification can be suggested:
1. simple
2. complex
3. very complex.

People can be asked to look at the various operations and to put them into one or other category.

It is true that if a worker gets used to a complex operation or

People who are not very
good at having new ideas
might be very good at
indicating where new
ideas are badly needed.

becomes good at it, then that person may no longer perceive it as complex. Indeed, that person may not even want to simplify the operation because he or she would lose the 'expert' status.

Existing suggestion schemes are obvious channels through which the ladder approach can be implemented. There is a need to emphasize the focus on 'simplicity'. There can also be a value in shifting the attention focus from month to month. So one month it may be 'simplicity in area A' and next month the request may be for 'simplicity in area B'.

As in all suggestion schemes it is useful to emphasize that suggested ideas should also show the 'benefit' of the idea and the 'practicality'. Too many creative people believe that 'clever novelty' is enough.

In addition to asking for simplifying ideas, it is also useful to ask people to 'pin-point' areas which need simplifying, areas which need some 'new thinking'. People who are not good at having new ideas might be very good at defining where creative thinking is needed. That is one of the reasons behind the success of Japanese suggestion schemes.

Is simplicity only a second-order value? If there is an apparent conflict between productivity and simplicity, which value should prevail? If simplicity suggests that a worker should take one step, but productivity seems to require three steps, what should the worker do?

Such a situation would be quite rare. The first thing would be to give some design attention to the situation instead of immediately treating it as an either/or situation. Can the productivity be retained

Simplicity and productivity are not in conflict. Simplicity leads through into productivity. Where there seems to be a conflict some design effort is needed.

and the simplicity introduced? What is the gain in productivity and what is the gain in simplicity? It should be remembered that simplicity also leads through to productivity in a number of ways:

1. less stress and anxiety
2. the possibility of working faster
3. increased safety
4. fewer errors
5. the job being done by less skilled people.

All these factors have to be taken into account before choosing productivity over simplicity. But the design effort has to come first. Why not have both productivity and simplicity?

_____

The small steps of the ladder approach are usually much easier to implement than the large steps of restructuring. The steps may even be within the 'decision space' of those making the suggestions.

The ladder approach can also serve to get people thinking in terms of simplification and change. This attitude can provide a useful background for the introduction of major structural changes which can also be shown to simplify matters. Once people are thinking 'simplification' and are in a simping mode, there might be less resistance to change.

The flavour approach

This approach is almost exactly the opposite of the ladder approach. Instead of the small steps of simplification that the ladder approach suggests, there is a very broad overview of the entire operation. This gets close to the 'start afresh' approach but is even more general than that. Flavours are real but indistinct and difficult to

In order to free ourselves from the constraints of what is now being done, we can start with a very broad approach to the whole purpose of the operation.

describe. So the flavour approach works from a very general base.

The purpose of education is to prepare youngsters to contribute to themselves and to society.

The purpose of welfare is to help those who cannot fully sustain themselves in society.

Ecology is about assessing the impact of an action or operation on the environment.

The purpose of the lawcourts is to assess the application of the law to individuals (or individual organizations).

The function of insurance is for all those exposed to a risk to contribute to the compensation of those who suffer damage as a result of the risk becoming a damaging reality.

The purpose of a hotel is to rent sleeping accommodation to those who cannot use their own.

The flavour approach frees the thinker completely from what is currently being done. This freedom is even greater than that enjoyed under the start-afresh approach.

Education might now be delivered by some sort of 'social apprenticeship' scheme, with individuals taking responsibility for groups of youngsters.

Welfare might now offer basic thinking skills and 'work design' rather than just money.

Ecology might now move as much into design as into judgement.

217

We are not trying to find
new approaches as such
but new approaches
which are simpler.
Simplicity is the value
being sought.

Guilt assessment might now pass through layers of probability before coming to full trial (with its delay and expenses).

Those who are exposed to a risk might invest and profit from a surplus of contributions.

The hotel might now function by organizing sleeping accommodation in private houses (with quality inspections).

Once you move to a very broad 'flavour' level, it becomes possible to open up totally new ways of doing things. Some of these might be interesting approaches in their own right. For the purpose of this book we are mainly interested in new approaches which offer greater simplicity.

So simplicity features both in the design of the new idea and also in the selection of those ideas which might be pursued further.

In itself, the flavour approach might give an idea that is much more complex than the existing idea. So it is important to keep simplicity in mind as a key value. It is important not to abandon simplicity in favour of other perceived benefits.

The purpose of an airline is to make profits out of the air travel of people (and goods).

From the flavour approach might come the idea of an airline which did not own planes and did not have its own schedule. This airline would simply take over certain flights and treat them as 'luxury flights' in much the same way as the Pullman Service operated on trains.

This is an interesting idea which might offer many benefits but it is hard to see it as a simplifying idea.

Ideas can evolve over time to achieve a form which no one would have wanted to design in the first place.

A simplifying idea might be to bundle all the needs of air travellers into one package and make profits from the different segments of the package (hotels, restaurants, car hire, guides, etc.).

Ideas evolve over time: to meet market demands; to take advantage of new technology; to adhere to new regulations. The result is sometimes an operation which no one would have designed in the first place. The flavour approach allows a total freedom of thinking in design.

Electricity is generally useful but may be dangerous. Motor-cars are generally useful but may be dangerous. A knife is generally useful but may be dangerous.

Chapter 12

The Dangers of Simplicity

If you put something simply, you are at the mercy of those who understand neither the subject nor simplicity.

Too simple

There must be dangers in simplicity otherwise why should we have invented so many words to describe things that are too simple:

simplistic
oversimplification
simplism
simple-minded
simpleton

It is just possible that some of these words were invented by pompous academics who did not believe that things should be made simple enough for ordinary folk to understand. After all, Martin Luther got into trouble for putting on the church door messages in ordinary German, which people could understand, instead of Latin, which they could not understand.

Time and again I have had pompous idiots look at some of my thinking 'tools' and declare them 'too simple to work'. Yet, in real life, they work very well.

———

One of the dangers I mentioned earlier, is that if you put something very simply, those who do not know the subject well have no option but to regard it as simplistic. This is a real danger.

The mirror image of this is that if you do not know the subject well, what you consider to be simple may indeed be 'simplistic'.

Since no one can know all subjects, it does become difficult to distinguish excellent simplicity from simplism.

———

The simplification process
can be taken too far,
giving a sort of anorexia
of simplicity.

Richness and complexity
are not the same thing.
Richness is a deliberate
choice – complexity is
merely an absence of
simplicity.

Oversimplification does exist. The danger of oversimplification is that certain important aspects, factors, elements or considerations are left out. The 'trade-off' between the value of simplicity and the value of comprehensiveness has swung too far in favour of simplicity. Here I am referring to the genuine simplification of someone who does know the subject and is striving to make an operation as simple as possible.

Even with this sort of oversimplification we do need to look 'forward' not 'backward'. The huge increase in the operacy (working usefulness) of something may compensate for the lack of comprehensiveness.

Anorexics are unfortunate people who take the slimming process so far that it becomes an obsession and a serious medical problem. It is possible to have a sort of 'anorexia of simplicity'.

Simple is boring

Some salt on food is very good. But few people put salt into their coffee or their fruit salad. (Salt *is* good on strawberries.) Because something is good and useful does not mean that it has the same value in all circumstances.

Provincial French cooking is simple and excellent. There may be times when the rich sauces of Parisian cooking are preferred.

In art there are times when the rich complexity of Gothic and Baroque are preferred to simplicity. There are hairstyles which are complex and hairstyles which are simple. Both can look very good.

Perhaps we need to distinguish very carefully between 'richness' and 'complexity'.

If you do not fit into any of the simple boxes you will be unfairly forced into one of them – or ignored completely.

Richness is intended to be its own value, just as a rich sauce is intended to be a rich sauce. The value lies in the blending of many flavours.

Complexity, as such, is not intended to be its own value. Complexity is a complex way of doing something where the value lies in what is being done, not in the way of doing it. Complexity is the absence of simplicity. Richness is the intended presence of richness.

There are times and there are circumstances where someone may genuinely prefer richness to simplicity. There are times when the richness of antique furniture is preferred to the slim lines of more modern furniture. There are times when the full 'Edwardian' proportions of a female figure are preferred to the slimness of catwalk models.

Simple is unfair

If the law had only a few simple categories, you might be forced into a category which was unfair on you. If the law had just one category for theft, then someone who stole a tie might be treated the same as an armed bank robber.

The complexity of laws and regulations grows in order to deal with exceptions and clever ways around existing regulations. The intention is 'fairness'.

If you design to deal only with the 'bulk' of cases then this is going to be unfair on the exceptions – unless you also design specifically to deal with the exceptions.

In education there is the bulk of students and then there are 'special' students at either end of the bell curve. There are the very gifted students who get bored and whose talents need developing. Such

As an idea develops it may go from simple to complex and then back to simple. Growth may be excluded if complexity is excluded.

talents are wasted in society if they are not developed (and taught thinking). At the other end are the students who are somewhat slower or who do not respond to the usual teaching methods. They need extra help or teaching in smaller classes.

There is always the danger that in the pursuit of simplicity a system may ignore special cases and those who do not fit standard categories.

Maybe all systems should have a 'flexibility unit' set up specifically to deal with special cases who do not fit elsewhere. Unfortunately, such a unit would be overwhelmed with demands, as almost everyone would consider himself or herself a 'special case'.

Simplicity may kill evolution

Sometimes a system starts off simple and then becomes more complex and then becomes simple once again. This can be a normal process of evolution and adaptation to change. If the 'complex' phase is disallowed, then that system may be unable to evolve or to adapt.

Ideas may become more complex as they seek to cover a wider range of situations. Then they become simpler again as some new underlying principle is discovered. That has been the history of science (and to a lesser extent of philosophy, where complexity itself is accorded a value).

If a system is kept rigidly simple because any deviation threatens the simplicity, then these adaptive changes may be excluded.

To be effective, communication must be simple and clear. Slogans that are simple and clear and build on existing prejudices have caused immense trouble in society.

Simplicity may not be commercial

From time to time someone produces a very short synopsis of all Shakespeare's plays.

Romeo and Juliet: Boy and girl love each other. Family problems. Through a misunderstanding both end up dead.

I have always preferred to write very short books, but publishers insist on a certain length in order to be able to charge a commercial price which covers all the work, handling, etc.

Supermarkets very rarely have clear signs as to where the different foods are stocked. This is partly deliberate. Research in the USA shows that 80 per cent of the purchases in a supermarket are 'impulse' purchases. If you knew exactly where to go and went there immediately you would not be exposed to temptations on the way.

Simplicity may be socially dangerous

Simple slogans are easy to pick up on, then repeat and come to believe. It is true that these slogans should really be called 'simplistic'.

'There is a loss of jobs because jobs are going overseas to countries where labour is cheaper.'

'Immigrants are taking our jobs because they are willing to work for less money.'

'All our troubles are due to that ... (race, religion, minority, etc.).

'The multinationals steal our resources and control our lives.'

In economics simple theories may do what they are supposed to do but cause a lot of damage in the process. A fire will kill vermin but may also burn down the house.

'There is an international conspiracy of financiers and bankers who upset economies in order to make money.'

'Women cannot reach the top levels in business because men make deals in the locker room.'

The dilemma is that communication does have to be simple and clear to be effective, so slogans do work. Some may contain a slight element of truth. Others simply build on existing emotions and prejudices.

Simplistic thinking of this sort has been a serious problem in society over the centuries. It has led to wars, persecutions, enmities, etc. It is difficult to see how you could ever get people to go to war without such slogans.

Simplicity may be economically dangerous

Scientists search for ever-simpler underlying principles. Economists are much tempted to do the same. But the economic system may be a very different system. There are many more interactive and feedback loops. So simple prescriptions may be dangerous. They may work in the intended way but in the process may cause a lot of damage that is difficult to repair. There are some who put 'monetarism' in this category. Yet it does work to reduce inflation.

In economics it is difficult to distinguish a theory that is valid from one which is simplistic. There are no laboratory tests that can be done. The econometric models are rarely exact enough replicas of the psychology of individual consumers and decision-makers.

You can only maximize on today, you cannot maximize on what tomorrow may bring. So simplification through shedding may make an organization vulnerable to changes.

Politics is never about right decisions – it is about multiple sensitivities.

Simplicity may be vulnerable

Robust and flexible systems often contain a lot of duplication and redundancy. If one part of the system is down, another part can take over. If one line of communication is blocked, then another line can be used.

Simplification, especially of the 'shedding' type, can get rid of all the superfluous duplication. This may be fine and efficient for the moment but if there are difficulties the system may not be able to cope.

You can only 'maximize' on the present moment in time. You cannot maximize on 'what may happen' later. So with downsizing and cost-cutting an organization may be made very efficient in terms of this moment in time, but be made vulnerable to changes. In addition there may no longer be resources to open up new directions and new ventures.

Simplicity may be insensitive

Business executives usually make poor politicians. A business executive sees the situation clearly (sometimes with the help of colleagues) and makes a clear and simple decision. Orders are given for this decision to be put into effect. It may be the best possible decision.

A business executive in politics tries to do the same thing. It may indeed be the best possible decision. But politics has more sensitivities than business: Will it be accepted? What will the press say? What about the opposition? Is it consistent with electoral promises? Does it favour one group over another? Politics is never a matter of making and using the best decisions.

The same may apply on a more personal level. Simple decisions

The simplest things are often the hardest to understand – because our minds keep racing off in the wrong directions.

may not fully take into account the sensitivities of others. In doing business in the Far East the matter of 'face' is a sensitivity most Western business executives find difficult to take into account.

Simplicity may be difficult to understand

This may seem a total nonsense. The purpose of simplicity is to make it easy to understand. In my experience, however, over many years of seminars and lectures, I have found that people have the most difficulty in understanding the simplest things.

This is because they cannot believe that something could be so simple. So they want to elaborate the matter with their own ideas and frameworks.

Furthermore, if something is simple, then people go chasing off in many different directions – most of which are incorrect. With something complex you are so challenged to understand it that you do not have the opportunity of chasing off in the wrong direction.

Something does not have
to be comprehensive to
be useful.

Useful things are things
which some people find
useful.

Chapter 13

Simple Notes on Everyday Simplicity

The human brain is perfectly capable of handling many things at the same time, but it is simpler to pay attention to one thing at a time when complexity is a problem.

Simple notes

There is nothing exotic or highly original about the notes put down here. The notes are by no means comprehensive and any reader could probably supplement them with his or her own experience and observations. The reader may or may not agree with some of the points.

Much of the book has been concerned with the simplification of operations, systems and organizations. This chapter is directly concerned with habits of mind that can help with 'everyday simplicity' – that is to say, the 'simping habit' as part of our normal thinking process.

One thing at a time

The human mind is perfectly capable of doing several things at the same time. When I am giving a seminar I am:

talking
thinking of what to say next
drawing continually on the overhead projector
observing the audience
thinking of other matters that I have to deal with that day.

There is nothing wrong with thinking of many things at the same time. But if you find that matters are getting too complex, then it is worth seeking to 'pay attention' to only one thing at any one time: 'This is what I am attending to right now.'

A cook may be cooking and talking at the same time. Most production workers do the same. Shop assistants are capable of serving you, carrying on two conversations and also answering the phone – all at the same time. Once again, if matters seem to be getting

Verbalizing forces
precision on thoughts
which are vague,
indistinct and apparently
complex.

You do not have to agree
with what you have just
said to yourself.

complex, then the instruction to yourself to do only one thing at a time has a simplifying effect. It is not that you cannot do more than one thing at a time – but you choose not to for the moment.

Verbalize

The subconscious is a wonderful place. All sorts of strange and complex matters are supposed to happen there. We are told that what we have in consciousness is only a vague copy of all that is going on in the subconscious or unconscious mind. Maybe this is all true. Certainly, apparent complexity is difficult to cope with while it remains out of consciousness.

The simple habit of talking to oneself can simplify matters. If you want to be more dignified you can call it 'verbalizing'. This means stating in ordinary language what seems to be going on.

If you find it difficult to make a decision you can verbalize that difficulty:

'I am finding it difficult to make this decision because . . .

. . . none of the alternatives are very attractive.

. . . I cannot decide between very attractive alternatives. I do not want to turn my back on any of them.

. . . although it seems the right decision, I suspect there will be difficulties later.

. . . because I do not want to upset that person.

. . . because I really need more information.'

You should be able to
explain to yourself, very
clearly and in words, why
you have made a
particular decision or
choice.

If you develop the habit of being honest with yourself, this process of verbalizing can give you some surprises. It can clarify and simplify why something seems complex and difficult.

———————

Exactly the same 'verbalizing' process can be used after you have made a decision. You tell yourself why you are making that particular decision or choice.

'I am making this choice (decision) because . . .

. . . I do not really like taking risks.

. . . I can go back on it later.

. . . it is the easiest choice.

. . . I am bored.

. . . I do not like being criticized.

. . . everyone has advised me to do this.

. . . it opens up opportunities.

. . . it is the cheapest option.

. . . it is the safest option.'

———————

Dealing with separate things as if they were one is a most common source of complexity.

As I wrote in an earlier book (*De Bono's Thinking Course*) the three main reasons behind any decision could be simplified to:

1. fear
2. greed
3. hassle.

In your verbalization as to why you are making that choice or decision you can tell yourself which of these three is dominant.

Once you have verbalized the reasons behind your decision you can live happily with those reasons – or revisit the matter if you are not happy.

Whenever you look back on the decision you can tell yourself: 'I made that decision for these reasons . . .'

Unbundle and untangle

There are Viking brooches with figures intertwined in a complex manner. Complexity can arise because we are trying to deal with more than one matter at the same time.

'There are two separate issues here. We ought to separate them out and deal with each one on its own.'

'There are several problems rolled into one with the homeless: there are those who cannot cope in a complex society; there are those who have suffered some misfortune; there are a few who like the nomadic life-style; there are kids who have run away from home to the big city and there are those who simply cannot afford housing.'

'We need to separate our dislike for the boss from the inefficient way this office is run.'

Analysis is seeking to divide something into its true component parts. You can also break something down into parts that are merely convenient to deal with.

While the whole task may seem impossibly complex, each small step can be simple and do-able.

Unbundling is not so much a matter of analysing or breaking something down, but of separating out what should be separate matters.

Analysis and breaking things down into parts

The whole purpose of analysis is to simplify life. Instead of seeking to deal with a complex matter we analyse it in order to identify the different known elements. Then we know how to deal with them.

When we analyse a problem we seek to find the cause of the problem. Once we have found the cause of the problem we can remove that cause, so solving the problem. When we cannot remove the cause we are more or less paralysed, because we may then have to design a way forward leaving the cause in place – and our educational traditions have prepared us for analysis but not for design. We are excellent at seeking 'what is' but very poor at designing 'what may be'.

Analysis seeks to separate out the real components. Breaking something down into parts simply means breaking it down into 'bite-sized' chunks. We can then deal with the chunks, one at a time. This 'breaking down' process is arbitrary and for the sake of convenience. It is convenient to deal with the pieces chosen. Just as you cut up a cake as you wish, so you divide up the situation as you wish.

Small steps

A daunting and complex task can be broken down into tiny steps. You take the first step and then you take the next step, and so on. A journey of a thousand miles starts with one step.

It is usually a matter of designing your own small steps.

I was once half-way up a historical monument in Mexico. I was standing on a ledge about six inches deep and about the equivalent of six storeys above the ground. It was frightening to go on, frightening to go back and impossible to just stay there. So I concentrated on just taking the next step and then the next step. In this way I climbed to the top of the building – and did the same thing on the way down.

It is always much simpler to focus on the next step than to focus on the entire task.

Sometimes the 'next steps' are obvious (as on the monument) but at other times you have to design the next steps. So you design the steps to be very small and easy to take. Climbers up Mount Everest take one step at a time. Sometimes they need to carve out the next step.

Use concepts

In our thinking we do not make nearly enough use of 'concepts'. We prefer to deal with concrete detail – because that is how we have been taught. Our minds, however, are dealing with concepts all the time. But we keep them out of sight in our subconscious. Concepts are a broad and general way of simplifying things.

Once you can extract a concept and verbalize it, you are well on the way to simplifying matters.

You are driving in the countryside and you get lost. So you use a broad concept to simplify matters:

'Keep driving north and sooner or later you will hit the motorway.'

That is simpler than seeking to examine each road and each junction you come to.

Concepts are the brain's way of simplifying the world and actions in the world. A concept is broad, blurry and vague enough to cover many possibilities.

The sales force is not performing well enough so you decide to offer them an 'incentive'. The details of the incentive will still need to be worked out but the broad direction of action is now set. You might have opted for the concept of 'training' or 'more marketing support'. In each case the concept simplifies the situation. That is exactly the purpose of concepts: to simplify action into stages. The first stage is to determine the concept and the second stage is to turn the concept into practical detail.

The concept of 'democracy' is important. So too are the practical details of how the concept is going to be implemented.

Thinking in stages

For some reason the human mind does not like 'dog-leg' thinking. We like to have the objective clearly in mind and then we figure out how to reach the objective. In dog-leg thinking we take a step in a direction which is apparently not that of the objective. When we have got to a new position, then, from that new position, we seek to move to the objective. This is supposed to be like the hind leg of a dog.

In one of my previous books (*The Mechanism of Mind*) I set the simple task of 'making a hole in a postcard big enough to put your head through'.

I suggested that you start off by cutting the postcard into a spiral. Obviously, this is not a satisfactory solution because a spiral has two ends and you are not allowed to join the ends. The next step is to cut down the centre of the spiral strip, stopping short of each end. You now have a hole big enough to put your head through. I illustrated this with a drawing of the different stages. This very much upset an eminent psychologist who was reviewing the book. I cannot think why, except that he was predisposed to be upset.

In dog-leg thinking you
do not move directly
towards the objective.
You move to a new
position from which
you seek to move to
the objective.

There were far more important things in the book to be upset about because the book described how the nerve networks acted as a self-organizing information system. I suspect he did not understand that part and so focused on a trivial issue.

In the provocative processes of lateral thinking we carry out dog-leg thinking. We put forward a provocation and then move on from it to a useful idea.

'Po: cars should have square wheels', does not seem an idea likely to improve the performance of cars.

From this provocation we move on to 'active suspension' or 'intelligent suspension': the suspension acts in anticipation of need. Such vehicles now exist.

'Po: bring back the town crier' was a provocation that led to the idea of free telephone calls paid for by inserted advertisements. This system is now in use in several countries.

This process of dog-leg thinking has some similarity to the well-known process in mathematics of converting a new problem to a familiar one for which the solution is known.

Working backwards

The human mind probably does not like dog-leg thinking because the mind likes 'working backwards'. We work backwards from where we want to reach with a succession of concepts which get more specific until finally we have a concrete idea we can use.

This process is formalized in the 'concept fan' technique of lateral thinking.

We work backwards from where we want to be to where we are now. The concepts get progressively more specific until we end up with concrete ideas.

What are the broad approaches or 'direction' which will take us to our objective?

What are the 'concepts' we can use in order to move in those broad directions?

What are the specific and concrete ideas that we can use to put those concepts into action?

If the problem was a shortage of trained staff then the directions could be:

. . . increase the supply of trained staff

. . . reduce the need for trained staff

. . . get more productivity out of the existing trained staff.

The concepts to serve the 'direction' of getting more productivity from existing staff might be:

. . . have them work harder

. . . make fuller use of their skill time.

The concrete ideas to implement the concept of making fuller use of their skill time might be:

. . . give them assistants to do all the work which does not need their special skill

. . . share them between different departments or even different organizations.

Each direction leads to a number of concepts. Each concept leads

Quite simple frameworks can make thinking much simpler. At any moment we know what we are trying to do at that moment.

to a number of ideas. So there is a cascade effect which multiplies the possible action alternatives.

Frameworks like this make thinking much simpler.

Parallel thinking

Instead of the primitive and crude argument method which often tends to make matters more complex there is the much simpler Six Hats method which makes use of parallel thinking (fully explained in *Six Thinking Hats* and *Parallel Thinking*).

At any one moment all parties are looking in the same direction and putting down their thoughts in parallel. There are six different directions, each of which is indicated by a different coloured 'hat'.

This extremely simple system is now widely in use in major corporations around the world and also in schools. The method shortens meeting times to a quarter or less of the time they usually take. It makes for thinking that is more constructive. It removes the ego battles from meetings.

The method also simplifies thinking by separating out each strand, which is then used on its own. The chemical balances in the brain make it impossible to handle all modes of thinking at the same time. John Culvenor in Australia wrote a research paper in which he showed that safety engineers taught the Six Hats method did twice as well in their own field as those not so taught.

There is no need to be perfect

If you try to be perfect the complexity of the task will overwhelm you. It may sometimes be enough to do a good job.

Errors are not acceptable
but the search for
ultimate perfection may
add more complexity
than it is worth.

If you set out to write a perfect book you would never get it done. It would take so long that by the time you had neared completion your ideas would have changed and you might have to start all over again.

Indicating that there is no need to be perfect does not mean an acceptance of errors. There should be zero tolerance of errors. It means that when something is error-free it can still be polished and polished and polished. This adds some extra value but introduces a lot of extra complexity.

Do things very slowly

When you feel oppressed by complexity it can help to do everything very, very slowly. This requires great discipline and great concentration. I suspect that the calming value of the Chinese Tai Chi exercises is exactly this. Doing things slowly helps the mind to clarify and simplify things. It is a form of meditation.

It may also be that if the mind is minimally occupied, as in doing normal things abnormally slowly, then it is more able to have new ideas. That is why many people report having good ideas while the mind is minimally engaged as in shaving, carrying out a hobby, etc. Concentrating on something other than what you are worried about can lead to thinking that is clearer and simpler.

Clarify

Clarity and simplicity go together. Putting on needed spectacles makes a confusing world less confusing.

What is the situation here?

What do we really need to do?

The mind may have
better ideas when it is not
trying to have better
ideas.

Clarity is simplicity of
perception.

What is going on?

Questions of this sort can help clarify matters. We can also add the 'verbalizing' habit mentioned earlier in this chapter. We answer those questions with a distinct verbalized answer.

Is the ultimate aim of simplicity to design a simple life?

How simple is a simple life?

Chapter 14

The Simple Life

Each of the approaches, methods and suggestions put forward in this book can as easily be applied to designing a simpler life as they can to designing a simpler anything. You just need to be clear about values, priorities and considerations.

Dreams and reality

There are many people who live a simple life because they have no choice at all.

There are some people who have deliberately chosen to live a simple life.

There are some people who genuinely yearn to live a simple life.

There are many people who dream of a simple life – as long as they never have to make it a reality.

There are many 'experts' on the simple life.

There are many books on 'the simple life'.

Any book on simplicity might be expected to have a long and more or less useful chapter on 'the simple life'. This book will not.

I am not an expert on 'the simple life'. Indeed, my life is so complex that I have had to become something of an expert on how to make a complex life somewhat less complex. I have many different projects in many fields in many countries around the world.

All the methods, approaches and processes outlined in this book can be used to 'design' a simple life. For example, the 'shedding' process suggests you shed those aspects which are no longer essential. The 'wishful thinking' approach suggests you mentally design the ideal life and then compare it with the one you have. Each of the approaches can be tried.

Above the level of
'survival' we are more
bullied and pressured by
opportunities than by
demands.

There is a complexity of
temptations and
opportunities generated
by a fear of boredom.

The complexity of life

In any system where 'stickiness' and 'unstickiness' are not symmetrical there is increasing complexity. In life we acquire responsibilities, habits, possessions, relationships, needs, etc., much more readily than we discard them. This is part of the richness and enjoyment of life – but it is also part of the complexity of life.

Projects once started have their own momentum and demands. If you learn to ski you will soon start to enjoy skiing. That means that for two weeks every year you will be compelled to go skiing. If you learn to play golf you will eventually become quite good. This means you have to pack your golf clubs whenever you go on holiday. If you develop a fine taste for wines then you will forever be spending more money on wine than you really need to.

We are continually 'bullied' by opportunities. A young man at a party sees an attractive young woman and feels he ought to get to know her. You read a good review of a play and feel you ought to go to see it. A restaurant is recommended by your friends – so you have to try it out. A holiday area becomes fashionable and everyone is talking about it – so you have to see it for yourself.

Above the level of 'struggling to survive' we are all far more pressured by opportunities than by other pressures.

Attraction of the simple life

The attraction of the simple life is that you are no longer bullied by opportunities and excitements. You get to enjoy simple things far more thoroughly. If you spend time in a remote area you gradually get to appreciate the people who live in that area. You no longer yearn to meet the latest literary sensation at a dinner

It is only when you have
a headache that not-
having-a-headache is such
a very high value.

party. You no longer worry that you have not been asked to be on a certain committee.

'Not having a headache' is the most important wish in the world when you have a severe headache. This probably applies even more strongly to being seasick. But when you do not have a headache and when you are not seasick do you go around saying, 'Isn't it wonderful I do not have a headache (am not being seasick)'?

So the attraction of a simple life seems strongest when it is most remote. I often say that I want to go and live on 'love and goat's cheese' on an island. (I do have an island.) No one ever believes me because they do not believe I would ever give up the projects in which I am interested. I do mean it. But I also suspect I might get bored.

There are people who have had the courage to follow these dreams and been very happy as a result. There are others who have tried it for a while and decided that the simple life was not for them.

Complexity of the simple life

Parkinson's law stated that 'work expands to fill the time allotted to it'. There should be a law of complexity which might go as follows:

'Sufficient complexity will always be created to fill the need for complexity.'

In the apparently 'simple life' of monasteries and convents there are layers of complexity in personal relationships, hierarchies, perceived slights, territorial disputes, etc. What may seem simple on the surface may be anything but simple below the surface.

Instead of just switching on the electricity you have to be concerned with more complex ways of getting light, warmth and coolness. This complexity protects you from being concerned with greater complexities.

What could be more simple than switching on the electricity and getting light, heat for cooking, heat for bodily warmth, refrigeration, etc. If you have to do all these things without electricity life does get much more complex. Making your own paper from rags is enjoyable but much more complex. If you grow all your own vegetables, they may taste much better but it is more complex than buying them from the supermarket.

The 'simple life' is not really that simple. But the complexity is under your control; the complexity may be enjoyable and engrossing; and there are things you do have to do. In a sense, because you have to do so many things that we normally take for granted, you do not have time for 'normal' distractions. You are sufficiently distracted by the mechanics of survival.

There are times when it has been fashionable to be a rebel, a drop-out, an anarchist, etc. This means someone who rejects the normal behaviour of society and wants to do his or her 'own thing'. Frequently those who reject the restricting norms of society enter into a new, and tougher, set of regulations. There is a 'uniform' for being a drop-out or a hippie. There is expected behaviour. You are expected to have very 'uniform' thoughts and to quote certain 'uniform' philosophers. At a music festival one day a young woman said to her companion: 'You are wearing a revoltingly clean shirt.'

There is absolutely nothing wrong with such behaviour. You need to signal to society, and to yourself, that you are 'dropping out'. You need to be recognizable by others who have the same feelings – why should 'dropping out' have to be lonely? You need to have certain subjects to talk about, etc.

In a simple life you are in
control of a chosen
complexity of survival
instead of being pressured
by the complexity of
opportunity and the
world around.

The simple life often means an exchange of one sort of complexity for another. The big difference is that you no longer 'have to do things' because others expect it – you now have to do things because you want to and you need to in order to survive.

There is no reason why the 'complexity of simplicity' should not be a preferred choice of the 'complexity of complexity'.

Craftsmen engage themselves in complex tasks. The complexity of those tasks often gives a simplicity to their lives.

Some rules do not have to be obeyed – but it is useful to keep them in mind.

The purpose of a rule may be to remind us of what lies behind that rule.

Chapter 15

The Ten Rules of Simplicity

To get simplicity you have to want to get it. To want to get simplicity you have to put a high value on simplicity.

Rule 1. You need to put a very high value on simplicity.

This seems simple enough. In fact very few people put a high value on simplicity. They put some value on simplicity but usually this is a 'second-order' value. An operation must be effective or an operation must save money. If that operation can also be simple that 'would be nice' – but only so long as the simplicity did not interfere with the other values. When things are highly complicated we do often wish for simplicity. But when things are not complicated we rarely strive to make something as simple as possible. Simplicity is not often treated as a prime objective. If you do not put a very high value on simplicity, then simplicity is unlikely to just happen.

Rule 2. You must be determined to seek simplicity.

You must be motivated and determined to make an active effort to make things more simple. It is not enough just to appreciate simplicity if it is there. You need to make things simple in an active way. Simplicity is not a peripheral luxury that is 'added on' to other things. The drive or motivation to simplify must come from your own attitude. This attitude should also be encouraged by the surrounding organization or the person who has set the design brief. It is necessary to invest time, thinking energy, design effort and money in trying to make things more simple. People quite like simplicity if it does not cost anything but are usually unwilling to invest resources in making something more simple.

Simplicity has to be designed. In order to design something you need to know exactly what you are dealing with and what you intend to achieve.

Not everything that is there really needs to be there.

Rule 3. You need to understand the matter very well.

You need to be very clear about what you are trying to do. You need to be very clear about values. You need to be very clear about the many considerations that have to be taken into account. If you are seeking to understand a situation or process you need to know that process very well. If you do not, then the result of your efforts will be 'simplistic' rather than simple. True simplicity comes from thorough understanding. Simplicity before understanding is worthless. It is simplicity after understanding that has a value.

Rule 4. You need to design alternatives and possibilities.

The emphasis is on 'design'. Analysis plays an important part in simplification but in the end you have to 'design' a way forward. That design process needs creativity and lateral thinking. It is not a matter of designing the 'one right way'. It is more a matter of designing alternatives and possibilities, and then selecting one of them. The first idea that comes to mind is very unlikely to be the best. That is why it is so important to go on thinking and to produce some further possibilities.

Rule 5. You need to challenge and discard existing elements.

Everything needs to be challenged. Everything needs to justify its continued existence. Systems and operations have a natural tendency to grow ever more complicated. Things which were needed at one time may be no longer needed. Where something cannot be justified then 'shed' it. If you wish to retain something for the sake of tradition let that be a conscious decision.

Modify if you can – start afresh if you cannot.

Concepts are the human mind's way of simplifying the world around.

Rule 6. You need to be prepared to start over again.

It is much easier, and tempting to try, to modify an existing operation or structure in order to make it simpler. Sometimes, however, you need to be able to start again from the beginning. Be clear about what you are trying to do and then set about designing a way to do it – ignoring the existing system entirely. This is more difficult, more expensive and less likely to be acceptable. So you will need to show the benefits of the suggested new system and explain why modification would never achieve the same benefits. This restructuring can apply to a whole operation or to part of it.

Rule 7. You need to use concepts.

Concepts are the way the human mind simplifies the world around. If you do not use concepts, then you are working with detail. It is impossible to move sideways from detail to detail. You need to go back to a concept and then find another way forward out of that concept. Concepts provide the first stage of thinking in setting the general direction and purpose. Once you have this then you can find alternative ways of delivering that concept with specific ideas and concrete detail. Remember that it is the precise purpose of concepts to be general, vague and blurry. That is how they work.

Rule 8. You may need to break things down into smaller units.

The organization of a smaller unit is obviously simpler than the organization of a large unit. The smaller units are themselves organized to serve the larger purpose. This process involves decentralization and delegation. In order to understand something you may need to break it down into smaller parts – through analysis or through convenience. Complex systems work best when there are

If simplicity is a real
value then you must be
prepared to trade off
other real values in
order to gain simplicity.

For whose sake is the
simplicity being designed?
Who is going to benefit
from the simplicity?

sub-systems, each of which has a simpler organization which is integrated into the whole (like the tiny cells in the human body).

Rule 9. You need to be prepared to trade off other values for simplicity.

A system that seeks to be totally comprehensive may be very complex. You may need to trade off that comprehensiveness for simplicity. Then you design a parallel system to deal with the exceptional cases. So long as errors remain unacceptable, you may need to trade off perfection for practical simplicity. Simplicity is a real value and you may need to give up some other values in order to obtain simplicity. This sort of trade-off requires a clear sense of values and priorities. It is usually not possible to have everything, so there has to be a choice between different values. It is important to be deliberate and conscious of the choices that are being made.

Rule 10. You need to know for whose sake the simplicity is being designed.

Is the simplicity being designed for the users (customers) of a system or for the operators (owners) of the system? Is the simplicity for ease of manufacture or for ease of maintenance? Is the simplicity for ease of operation or for cost-saving? A shift of complexity may mean that a system is made very much easier for the customer but much more complicated for the operator. It more often happens the other way round. Who is supposed to benefit from this simplification? If everyone is not going to benefit, who is going to benefit?

Complexity harms everyone. So simplicity is everyone's business. So why not let everyone help out?

The Edward de Bono National Simplicity Campaign (and local campaigns)

Sometimes general feelings need to be made concrete through specific events or actions. The suggested 'Simplicity Campaign' is an attempt to do this for the wish for simplicity.

Intention

It is hoped to integrate this book into National Simplicity Campaigns. This would involve a partnership with national newspapers, radio or television stations. It might also involve a partnership with other organizations that see a value in simplicity. These things take time and may or may not happen in different countries. For example, in Australia, the campaign would be run by the De Bono Institute, which has been set up in Melbourne with funding from the Andrews Foundation.

In parallel with the national campaigns there can also be local campaigns, which are run in co-operation with a local radio station or local newspaper. These can be set up whether or not there is a national campaign. It is also possible to set up a simplicity campaign within a single organization, whether this is a business corporation, a public-service body or even a school. The framework for such a local campaign is given here. Local or mini campaigns do not have to await national campaigns.

The name

For the sake of coherence and so that all the local campaigns are seen as part of an overall campaign the name used should be:

The Edward de Bono Simplicity Campaign.

This also ensures that the principles put forward here are being followed. In addition, the name has a certain marketing and credibility value at this point in time. The association with lateral thinking is very relevant.

Simplicity campaigns can be organized nationally, locally in a community or within a particular organization. There will also be an Internet campaign.

Anyone wishing to organize such a simplicity campaign should write to me, giving details or background and plans, and I shall issue a simple licence (at no charge) for the use of the name (see page i for contact information). The name is a 'brand image' rather than a territorial franchise. The use of the name by one party does not exclude a use by other parties even in the same area.

The campaign

Members of the public (or a local community or an organization) are invited to submit ideas for 'simplification'. The following text can be used as part of this invitation.

'The world is getting ever more complex. Procedures and operations get more complex all the time. All this creates anxiety, frustration, difficulty and mental strain. You sometimes need to be a near-genius to do the simplest things. There seem to be many people making things more complex but very few people trying to make them simpler. This campaign is an invitation to you to become one of the people making things simpler. Everyone has a lot of brainpower – if they choose to use it. You are now invited to focus that brainpower on making things simpler.

Edward de Bono'

The above can be part of the invitation to join the campaign – but does not have to be. The invitation may be issued through newspaper, radio, notice-board, in-house publications, etc. I, myself, shall be running a campaign on the Internet at http://www.edwdebono.com/

Not everyone feels able to have creative ideas. But everyone can point to something which badly needs to be done in a much simpler way. Everyone who has suffered from complexity knows exactly where the pain is.

The tasks

There are two separate tasks. You can try either or both, or submit entries in both classes.

Task A
You are invited to point to an area which seems to you to be too complex. You put your finger on an area that needs to be made simpler. It may be a procedure, a regulation or a way of doing things. You simply say: 'This thing (area, matter or procedure) needs to be made much simpler.' You do not need to say how it should be made simpler. It is enough that you indicate an area that needs to be made simpler. That is a high value in itself. You should not put forward ideas on how to make the matter simpler. Such ideas are part of Task B. It is enough just to indicate the complex area.

You do need to describe why the area you have chosen is complex. You should not assume that the person reading your entry will know all about it. So please describe how the area (or matter) is complicated. This is important. 'It is too complicated because . . .'

Task B
Here you are invited to submit ideas on how something could be made 'simpler'. This task requires you to do some creative thinking in order to offer a simpler way of doing things. You are invited to submit suggestions which would make things simpler. In Task A it was enough to point to the complicated area. In Task B you are expected to put forward practical and simple suggestions: 'We could do it this way . . .'

Suggestions for a simpler way to do something should be: simple, effective, practical and acceptable.

An approach which is simpler but does not do what it needs to do is not much use.

In carrying out Task B you will need to keep the following steps in mind.

1. Spell out why the existing method is complex (do not assume that the reader or judge will know all about it).

2. Put forward your simplifying suggestion as clearly as you can.

3. Spell out the benefits, the practicality and the possible acceptance of your suggestion.

4. Spell out the disadvantages and possible difficulties with your suggestion.

5. Suggest practical action steps to put your suggestion to work.

Your entry must be legible, otherwise the value of your thinking will be lost. This means typing, upper-case letters or legible handwriting. Entries should be as brief as possible and never more than one page.

Task A and Task B are quite separate and may be judged separately. So if you wish to submit the same matter for both tasks, each entry must be complete in itself – do not ask the judges to refer back to your Task A entry.

Judgement

A local panel of judges will need to be set up. Where necessary a technical suggestion can be referred to an expert in that field.

It is useful for those submitting ideas to know the basis on which those ideas are going to be evaluated.

The judges may choose to select a winner and a runner-up. The judges may choose to select a winner and several 'honourable mentions'. Where the campaign is run by a newspaper or radio station there may be 'the best idea of the week'. There are many possible variations.

Judgement would be on the basis of the following guidelines:

For Task A
1. The basic importance of the area pin-pointed. For example, how to organize emergency services may be more important than where to put a dog when visiting the supermarket. Importance may also refer to 'how many people are affected'. Something which affects many people every day is important even though it may seem trivial in itself.

2. The existing degree of complication in the process, area or matter. It is not enough that someone should suggest that something should be 'improved'. Everything should be improved. It is necessary to point out the complexity of things as they now exist. The more complex the matter the higher the value of the submission.

3. The clarity and simplicity with which all this is expressed.

For Task B
1. The 'power' of the simplicity of the idea. A really simple suggestion is going to win over a minor simplification. The change brought about by the simplification must be substantial. Change for the sake of change does not have a high value.

A powerful idea which is also accompanied by practical action steps for the implementation of the idea is more valuable than an idea which is left in theoretical space.

2. The effectiveness of the idea. Would the idea really work? Does the suggested alternative do all that is needed, all that was being done before? A suggestion that simplifies matters by only doing half the job is not of high value.

3. The practicality of the idea. Can the new idea be put into action? An idea that depends on some new, as yet uninvented, technology does not have a high value. The idea must be do-able with today's technology. The cost of the suggestion is also important. A suggestion that would involve large expenditures is not very practical in most cases.

4. The clarity and honesty with which the benefits and disadvantages of the suggestion are spelled out is a factor in the judgement of the idea. So also is the assessment of the 'acceptance' of the idea. Will all the people who will be using the idea be ready to accept the idea?

5. A high value will be given by the judges to the 'practical action steps' that could be taken to implement the idea.

In short, the judges will give high marks to ideas that are:

simple
effective
practical.

Contribution is sometimes a reward in itself. Recognition of the value of an idea is a further reward. The challenge of involvement and achievement are also satisfying.

Awards and rewards

The winners of the campaigns will have the reward of seeing their suggestions published as winning suggestions under their name. Where possible, more suggestions will be published than just those of the winners.

Local organizers may also decide on additional rewards, possibly sponsored by local corporations. 'Hero status' should be given to winners, as Du Pont does with creative people.

Winners might be given copies of this book, other books or the two very simple games (the L-game and the 3-Spot game) – for details see the information on page 49.

If it proves feasible, the winners or a short list can be submitted to me and I shall make a special award of a certificate or a 'de Bono medal'. This depends entirely on volume and practicalities.

The person who submits an idea retains full rights to that idea. If the idea is one that could be registered or patented, that will be the responsibility of the person submitting the idea. It should be remembered that many people will have similar ideas and should not be accused of 'stealing' them!

If the quality of ideas is high enough, then there might be a compilation of such suggestions as a published book.

All the above are possibilities, not promises. Much will depend on how the suggestion of simplicity campaigns is taken up.

Hunters are usually given specific seasons in which to hunt. Hunters for simpler ideas may benefit from the focus of a specific 'thinking' season.

Duration and frequency

The duration and frequency of the simplicity campaigns will depend a lot on the setting. A campaign within a corporation could run over several months with a different specific focus each week. A national or local campaign run by a newspaper or radio station might run over six weeks with the best entries being published each week and reminders given each week. It would also be possible to run a very short campaign lasting no more than two weeks. In such a case the selection and publication of winning entries would occur some time after the end of the two-week submission period.

The campaign could be a one-off event or could be repeated each year for a defined period.

There might even be a yearly 'Simplicity Day' when everyone puts their thoughts to making something simpler.

There are many possible variations.

Use of material

The material put forward here is part of the copyright of this book. A special licence to use this material can be applied for. There would be no charge for non-commercial use. Commercial use would need to be negotiated. There is a need for more simplicity in the world. There is a need for more people to make an effort to simplify matters. The suggested simplicity campaigns are a step in that direction.

PENGUIN ONLINE

READ MORE IN PENGUIN

In every corner of the world, on every subject under the sun, Penguin represents quality and variety – the very best in publishing today.

For complete information about books available from Penguin – including Puffins, Penguin Classics and Arkana – and how to order them, write to us at the appropriate address below. Please note that for copyright reasons the selection of books varies from country to country.

In the United Kingdom: Please write to *Dept. EP, Penguin Books Ltd, Bath Road, Harmondsworth, West Drayton, Middlesex UB7 ODA*

In the United States: Please write to *Consumer Sales, Penguin Putnam Inc., P.O. Box 12289 Dept. B, Newark, New Jersey 07101-5289.* VISA and MasterCard holders call 1-800-788-6262 to order Penguin titles

In Canada: Please write to *Penguin Books Canada Ltd, 10 Alcorn Avenue, Suite 300, Toronto, Ontario M4V 3B2*

In Australia: Please write to *Penguin Books Australia Ltd, P.O. Box 257, Ringwood, Victoria 3134*

In New Zealand: Please write to *Penguin Books (NZ) Ltd, Private Bag 102902, North Shore Mail Centre, Auckland 10*

In India: Please write to *Penguin Books India Pvt Ltd, 11 Community Centre, Panchsheel Park, New Delhi 110017*

In the Netherlands: Please write to *Penguin Books Netherlands bv, Postbus 3507, NL-1001 AH Amsterdam*

In Germany: Please write to *Penguin Books Deutschland GmbH, Metzlerstrasse 26, 60594 Frankfurt am Main*

In Spain: Please write to *Penguin Books S. A., Bravo Murillo 19, 1° B, 28015 Madrid*

In Italy: Please write to *Penguin Italia s.r.l., Via Benedetto Croce 2, 20094 Corsico, Milano*

In France: Please write to *Penguin France, Le Carré Wilson, 62 rue Benjamin Baillaud, 31500 Toulouse*

In Japan: Please write to *Penguin Books Japan Ltd, Kaneko Building, 2-3-25 Koraku, Bunkyo-Ku, Tokyo 112*

In South Africa: Please write to *Penguin Books South Africa (Pty) Ltd, Private Bag X14, Parkview, 2122 Johannesburg*

BY THE SAME AUTHOR

Parallel Thinking

'His boldest attempt yet to change the way our minds work' *Financial Times.* For two and a half thousand years we have followed the thinking system designed by Socrates, Plato and Aristotle, based on analysis, judgement and argument. In today's rapidly changing world, judgement and argument can no longer solve problems or move us forward. We need to switch from judgement to design. Dr de Bono shows how we can design forward from 'parallel possibilities'.

The Use of Lateral Thinking

This is Edward de Bono's original portrayal of a mental process which he in no way claims to have invented. In it he deliberately uses the lateral approach (with intriguing visual examples in one chapter) to sketch in the nature of lateral thinking. Imaginative, free-wheeling, opportunistic (but low-probability), lateral thinking is thus contrasted with the orthodox, logical, unimaginative (but high-probability) process of vertical thinking, from which it differs as a bus differs from a tram. In a changing world both modes are required.

Edward de Bono's Masterthinker's Handbook

It is never enough just to want to think or to exhort someone to think. What are the steps? What is to be done? Avoiding error and winning arguments are only a tiny part of thinking. The main enemies of thinking are confusion, inertia and not knowing what to do next. The 'Body' framework designed by Dr de Bono overcomes these problems.

Teaching Thinking

Even as little as seven hours' instruction in thinking can have a significant effect on performance. Teaching knowledge is not enough – in order to survive and thrive in a complex world every youngster leaving school needs to be equipped with basic thinking skills.

BY THE SAME AUTHOR

Handbook for the Positive Revolution

There are many people who have felt that negativity is not enough. They see the need to be constructive, to be creative and to contribute towards making things happen. These are the people who will welcome the Positive Revolution. Edward de Bono's challenging book provides a practical framework for a serious revolution which has no enemies but seeks to make things better.

Lateral Thinking

'Thinking' says Edward de Bono, 'is a skill, and like a skill it can be developed and improved if one knows how.' This book is a textbook of creativity. It shows how the habit of lateral thinking can be encouraged, and new ideas generated, by special techniques, in groups or alone. The result is a triumph of entertaining education.

Po: Beyond Yes and No

Most of us are trapped within the rigid confines of traditional ways of thinking, limited by concepts which have developed simply for the purposes of arriving at the 'right' answer. Edward de Bono offers Po as a device for changing our ways of thinking: a method of approaching problems in a more creative way.

Water Logic

To make problem-solving easier, Dr de Bono puts forward a visual 'flowscape' which allows us to see at a glance the important points and relationships. This 'flowscape' is based on water logic. Traditional 'rock logic' is based on identity: 'What is . . .?'. Water logic is based on 'flow': 'What does this lead to?'. If you want to simplify your thinking about complex issues, you need this book.

BY THE SAME AUTHOR

Atlas of Management Thinking

Research work on the brain has suggested that our usual thinking, dominated by language and logic, takes place on the left side of the brain. This book provides a repertoire of non-verbal images for the right side of the brain, so that you can add some right-brain thinking to your usual left-brain thinking!

Lateral Thinking for Management

Edward de Bono shows here how he sees creativity and lateral thinking working together in the process of management to develop new products and new ideas, and to generate new approaches to problem-solving, organization and future alternatives in planning.

The Happiness Purpose

Edward de Bono presents his blueprint for the disciplined pursuit of happiness, which is, in his opinion, the legitimate purpose of life. Self-respect, dignity, self-importance and humour occupy an important place in his scheme, and he shows how to utilize these assets as tools for mental and spiritual betterment.

Opportunities

'An opportunity is as real an ingredient in business as raw material, labour or finance – but it only exists when you can see it.' This handbook offers a systematic approach to opportunity-seeking at both corporate and executive levels. Remember: 'Just before it comes into existence every business is an opportunity that someone has seen.'

Conflicts

The usual negotiating methods used to resolve conflicts in the West are compromise and consensus. Here Edward de Bono puts forward an approach that involves making a map of the conflict 'terrain' and then using lateral thinking to generate alternative solutions.

BY THE SAME AUTHOR

Six Thinking Hats

'Thinking is the ultimate human resource', and yet most people make no efforts to improve. Edward de Bono shows us how to streamline our minds with six thinking hats: put on a black hat for a critical viewpoint, or yellow for sunny optimism; a green hat brings a wealth of creative ideas; try white for neutrality and red for emotion; then a sky-blue hat will give you a detached overview to sort out the range of possible solutions. The results will prove amazingly effective.

I Am Right – You Are Wrong

Edward de Bono puts forward a direct challenge to rock logic based on rigid categories, absolutes, argument and adversarial point scoring. Instead he proposes the water logic of perception. Drawing on our understanding of the brain as a self-organizing information system, Dr de Bono shows that perception is the key to more constructive thinking and the serious creativity of design.

Wordpower

Could you make an educated guess at the downside-risk of a marketing strategy? Are you in the right ball-game, and faced with a crisis, could you find an ad hoc solution? Would you recognize a catch-22 situation? These are just a few of the 265 'thinking chunks' defined here so that the reader can use them as powerful tools of expression.

Practical Thinking

How is it that in an argument both sides are always right? How is it that no one ever makes a mistake on purpose but that mistakes get made? These are some of the questions answered in this book, where de Bono's theme is how the mind actually works – not how philosophers think it should work.

BY THE SAME AUTHOR

How to be More Interesting

Some people are born intelligent. Some people are born beautiful. Some people are born strong. While we cannot do very much about strength, intelligence and beauty, being 'interesting' is entirely up to you. It is about playing with ideas, making connections, speculating and imagination. This book explains how to turn your mind into a playground of interest, with seventy exercises for you to practice your growing skill. Add in 'humenes' – the elements of humour, insight and surprise – and everybody is guaranteed to find you interesting!

Edward de Bono's Textbook of Wisdom

Some people wait for grey hair in the hope this will automatically impart wisdom. Others will read this book, which is a presentation of 'thinking tools', guidelines and principles. Edward de Bono recognizes that our brains deserve and demand that we do better with them, and uses his gift for clarity and simplicity to get readers' thoughts to flow along fresh, contemporary lines.

Teach Yourself to Think

Thinking is the most fundamental skill – your happiness and your success depend upon it. In this book is a clear and effectively simple five-stage framework for thinking: the TO stage (where am I going to?); the LO stage (looking around at the situation); the PO stage (generating possibilities); the SO stage (choosing from the possibilities); and finally, the GO stage (going ahead and putting thinking into action).

Teach Your Child How to Think

Edward de Bono shows in a simple and practical way how a parent can develop the thinking skills of his or her children so as to give them a better chance in life. Today's world demands clear and constructive thinking: the ability to make decisions, to plan initiatives and be creative. Even a single thinking habit taken from this comprehensive book may strongly affect the future of your child.